Philosophy of Bhagavad Gita

Devendra Kumar

I

Preface

The *Bhagavad Gita*, often called the *Song of God*, is one of the most profound spiritual and philosophical texts in human history. Rooted in the great epic *Mahabharata*, it is a timeless dialogue between Lord Krishna and Arjuna on the battlefield of Kurukshetra. This divine conversation transcends time, culture, and religion, offering deep insights into life's most fundamental questions—duty, morality, righteousness, self-realization, and the path to liberation.

The essence of the *Bhagavad Gita* lies in its ability to provide wisdom that is both universal and practical. Whether one is a seeker of truth, a leader facing ethical dilemmas, or an individual striving for inner peace, the teachings of the Gita remain eternally relevant. It teaches us how to perform our duties selflessly, maintain equanimity amidst life's uncertainties, and transcend material attachments to attain spiritual fulfillment.

This book, *Philosophy of Bhagavad Gita*, aims to explore the deeper philosophical meanings embedded within the Gita's verses. It delves into key concepts such as Dharma (righteous duty), Karma (action and consequence), Yoga (paths to liberation), and Atman (the eternal self). Additionally, it connects these teachings to modern life, demonstrating their significance in personal, professional, and societal contexts.

In a world filled with stress, uncertainty, and moral conflicts, the Bhagavad Gita serves as a guiding light. It does not advocate renunciation of the world but rather teaches us how to live within it with wisdom, devotion, and purpose. As we embark on this journey through the Gita's timeless wisdom, may it inspire us to lead a life of balance, clarity, and self-realization.

Contents

This book will provide a structured exploration of the *Bhagavad Gita*'s timeless wisdom, offering insights that remain as relevant today as they were thousands of years ago. Stay tuned as we delve deeper into each concept and its practical applications.

"Whatever happened, happened for the good. Whatever is happening, is happening for the good. Whatever will happen, will happen for the good." — Bhagavad Gita

Chapter 01: Introduction

1 Historical and Literary Context of Bhagavad Gita

The **Bhagavad Gita**, often referred to as the "Song of the Divine," is one of the most profound and revered scriptures in Hindu philosophy. It is a 700-verse dialogue between **Lord Krishna and Arjuna**, set on the battlefield of **Kurukshetra**, where Arjuna faces a deep moral and existential crisis. The Gita is a part of the great epic **Mahabharata** and is believed to have been composed between **5th and 2nd century BCE**, though its teachings remain timeless. It integrates various philosophical traditions, including **Vedanta, Samkhya, and Yoga**, while addressing the eternal dilemmas of **duty, righteousness, and self-realization**. The Bhagavad Gita is not merely a religious text but a **universal guide to life, action, and spiritual wisdom**, influencing countless philosophers, leaders, and spiritual seekers across the world.

Historical Background and Development

The Bhagavad Gita emerged during a period of significant socio-political and philosophical transformation in ancient India. The era of its composition was marked by the **rise of diverse philosophical schools, the decline of Vedic ritualism, and the emergence of new spiritual and ethical thought systems.**

Vedic Roots and Upanishadic Influence

The **Vedas**, the oldest sacred texts of Hinduism, form the foundation of Indian spirituality. The Rigveda and Yajurveda laid emphasis on cosmic order (**Rta**), duty (**Dharma**), and sacrificial rituals (**Yajna**). However, as society evolved, the ritualistic approach of the Vedas gave way to **philosophical introspection**, as seen in the **Upanishads**, which introduced **monistic (Advaita) and dualistic (Dvaita) concepts of reality**. The Upanishadic teachings emphasized **Brahman (the absolute reality), Atman (the individual soul), and Moksha (liberation)**, ideas that became central to the Bhagavad Gita.

The Bhagavad Gita synthesizes these Upanishadic teachings with the earlier Vedic ideas, transforming them into a more **practical and action-oriented philosophy**. While the Upanishads focus on renunciation and introspection, the Gita integrates **engaged spirituality**—the idea that one can attain liberation while fulfilling worldly responsibilities.

The Mahabharata and the Kurukshetra Context

The Bhagavad Gita is embedded within the **Mahabharata**, the great Sanskrit epic attributed to **Sage Vyasa**. The Mahabharata itself is a vast literary and philosophical work that reflects the socio-political conflicts and ethical dilemmas of its time. The setting of the Gita on the battlefield of **Kurukshetra** is symbolic—it represents the larger struggle of life, where one must confront dilemmas of **right and wrong, action and inaction, duty and personal attachment**.

Arjuna's moral dilemma before the war encapsulates the universal human experience of **confusion, doubt, and ethical crisis**. His refusal to fight against his own kin reflects a deep existential conflict, which Krishna resolves by expounding the eternal principles of **Dharma, Karma, and Bhakti**.

Philosophical Contributions and Schools of Thought

The Bhagavad Gita stands at the confluence of several philosophical traditions. It draws from the **Samkhya, Yoga, and Vedanta schools of Indian thought**, presenting a comprehensive view of life, action, and transcendence.

Samkhya Philosophy and its Role

Samkhya, attributed to **Sage Kapila**, is one of the oldest philosophical systems in India. It postulates a dualistic reality where **Purusha (consciousness) and Prakriti (matter)** are distinct. The Gita integrates Samkhya ideas but modifies them—unlike classical Samkhya, which is non-theistic, the Gita presents Krishna as the **Supreme Purusha**, transcending both matter and consciousness.

Krishna explains that **the soul (Atman) is eternal, indestructible, and beyond the material world**. While the body perishes, the soul moves through cycles of birth and rebirth until it attains liberation.

The Path of Yoga: Action, Knowledge, and Devotion

The Bhagavad Gita introduces three primary **paths to liberation (Moksha)**:

1. **Karma Yoga (Path of Selfless Action)** – Advocates performing one's duty without

attachment to results. Krishna teaches Arjuna that **action performed without selfish motives leads to liberation.**

2. **Jnana Yoga (Path of Knowledge)** – Emphasizes self-inquiry and realization of the **non-duality between Atman and Brahman**.

3. **Bhakti Yoga (Path of Devotion)** – Highlights the importance of surrendering to the **divine will (Krishna)** through faith and devotion.

These three paths reflect an **inclusive and dynamic approach to spirituality**, making the Gita accessible to people of all temperaments.

Ethical and Metaphysical Teachings

The Bhagavad Gita presents profound ethical and metaphysical teachings that remain relevant in philosophical discourse.

The Concept of Dharma (Duty) and Righteous Action

A central theme of the Gita is **Dharma (righteous duty).** Unlike rigid moral codes, Dharma is **context-dependent**—it varies based on one's role and responsibilities in life. For Arjuna, as a Kshatriya (warrior), his Dharma is to fight for justice, even against his own relatives.

Krishna teaches **Nishkama Karma (selfless action),** emphasizing that **one must act according to duty without attachment to success or failure**. This concept influenced later Indian philosophical and ethical thought, including Gandhi's principle of **detached action** in non-violent resistance.

The Three Gunas: Sattva, Rajas, and Tamas
The Bhagavad Gita describes the **three Gunas (modes of material nature):**

- **Sattva (purity, wisdom, harmony)** – Leads to enlightenment and inner peace.

- **Rajas (passion, desire, activity)** – Fuels ambition but also attachment.

- **Tamas (ignorance, inertia, darkness)** – Results in delusion and stagnation.

Krishna advises **transcending these Gunas through spiritual wisdom and self-discipline**.

The Vision of the Supreme Reality (Brahman and Maya)
The Gita's metaphysical insights bridge **duality and non-duality**, addressing the **relationship between the finite and the infinite**. Krishna reveals that **while the world appears real (Maya), ultimate reality (Brahman) transcends it**. This idea is central to **Advaita Vedanta**, which teaches the unity of the individual soul (Atman) and the supreme reality (Brahman).

Global Influence and Comparative Philosophy

The Bhagavad Gita has influenced thinkers across **India and the world**.

Influence on Indian Thinkers
- **Adi Shankaracharya** interpreted the Gita through the lens of Advaita Vedanta.

- **Swami Vivekananda** saw it as a guide to self-reliance and fearlessness.

- **Mahatma Gandhi** considered the Gita his **spiritual dictionary**, shaping his principles of non-violence and detached action.

Western Engagement with the Gita
- **Schopenhauer** admired its metaphysical depth.

- **Aldous Huxley** referenced it in his work on **perennial philosophy**.

- **Carl Jung** explored its psychological insights on self-realization.

Conclusion

The Bhagavad Gita remains one of the most influential philosophical texts, bridging **ethics, metaphysics, and spirituality**. Its universal themes of **duty, knowledge, devotion, and liberation** continue to inspire people across generations. Whether viewed as a **spiritual guide, a philosophical treatise, or an ethical manual**, the Gita's wisdom transcends time and culture, offering profound insights into **the nature of life, self, and ultimate reality**.

2 Overview of the 18 Chapters of the Bhagavad Gita

The **Bhagavad Gita**, a sacred Hindu scripture and part of the great epic **Mahabharata**, consists of 18 chapters, each providing deep philosophical and ethical insights. The Gita unfolds as a conversation between **Lord Krishna** and **Arjuna** on the battlefield of **Kurukshetra**, addressing the dilemmas of duty, righteousness, devotion, and self-realization. Below is an overview of its 18 chapters, explaining their core teachings and philosophical significance.

Chapter 1: Arjuna Vishada Yoga (The Yoga of Arjuna's Dejection)

The first chapter of the **Bhagavad Gita**, known as **Arjuna Vishada Yoga**, sets the stage for the profound discourse between **Lord Krishna and Arjuna**. This chapter introduces the battlefield of **Kurukshetra**, where the great war between the **Pandavas and Kauravas** is about to begin. The scene is intense, with warriors from both sides preparing for battle, conch shells being blown, and the atmosphere charged with anticipation. **King Dhritarashtra**, the blind ruler of the Kuru dynasty, inquires from **Sanjaya**, his charioteer and divine seer, about the happenings on the battlefield. Sanjaya, blessed with divine vision, describes the scene vividly, narrating how the Pandava prince **Arjuna** requests Lord Krishna, his charioteer, to place his chariot between the two armies so he can see who he is about to fight.

As Arjuna surveys the battlefield, he is overcome with deep sorrow and moral conflict. He sees his **relatives, revered elders, teachers, and friends** on both sides, all prepared for battle. The sight of his own family members standing against him shakes him to his core. **Compassion and attachment** overwhelm his warrior spirit, and he is gripped by **doubt, fear, and helplessness**. Arjuna questions the very purpose of the war, arguing that victory at the cost of **slaughtering his kin** would bring him no joy. He fears that such a war would lead to the destruction of family traditions (**Kuladharma**), moral decline, and social chaos. He argues that a war fought for personal or political gains would result in nothing but sin.

Overcome by despair, Arjuna **drops his bow and arrows**, refusing to fight. He turns to Krishna, seeking guidance but still unwilling to take action. This chapter is crucial as it marks **the beginning of Arjuna's spiritual journey**, where he transitions from a state of **moral confusion and emotional turmoil to seeking wisdom and clarity**. The chapter ends with Arjuna surrendering himself to Krishna's counsel, paving the way for the **profound teachings of the Bhagavad Gita** in the following chapters. **Arjuna Vishada Yoga represents the universal human dilemma—moral confusion, emotional distress, and the search for meaning amidst life's greatest challenges.**

Chapter 2: Sankhya Yoga (The Yoga of Knowledge)

Chapter 2 of the **Bhagavad Gita**, known as **Sankhya Yoga**, is one of the most significant chapters, as it lays the philosophical foundation for the entire text. After witnessing Arjuna's deep despair in Chapter 1, Lord Krishna begins his teachings, addressing Arjuna's confusion and sorrow with profound wisdom. Krishna rebukes Arjuna for his weakness, reminding him that his grief is **unworthy of a warrior (Kshatriya)** and that true wisdom lies in understanding the eternal nature of the self (**Atman**).

Krishna introduces **the concept of the immortal soul (Atman),** explaining that while the body is perishable, the soul is eternal, indestructible, and beyond birth and death. He tells Arjuna that just as a person changes clothes, the soul discards an old body and takes on a new one, undergoing cycles of **birth and rebirth (Samsara).** Therefore, grieving for the inevitable is **ignorance**, and true wisdom lies in detachment from bodily identification.

Krishna then introduces **Karma Yoga (the path of selfless action)**, teaching Arjuna the importance of performing his duty (**Dharma**) without attachment to success or failure. He emphasizes the principle of **Nishkama Karma**, meaning **one should act without desiring the fruits of action**. Krishna explains that attachment to results leads to bondage, whereas selfless action performed with equanimity leads to spiritual liberation (**Moksha**).

He also describes **Sankhya Yoga (the path of knowledge),** which involves discerning the difference between the **eternal soul and the temporary material world**. Krishna encourages Arjuna to cultivate **Stitha-Prajna (steady wisdom)**—a state where one remains unaffected by pleasure and pain, success and failure, attachment and aversion. A **self-realized person** is one who transcends material desires, is free from ego, and remains absorbed in the divine consciousness.

The chapter concludes with Krishna urging Arjuna to rise above his doubts, embrace his duty as a warrior, and fight with **courage, wisdom, and devotion. Sankhya Yoga provides a comprehensive guide to self-realization, teaching that knowledge, detached action, and inner stability are the keys to true freedom.**

Chapter 3: Karma Yoga (The Yoga of Action)

Chapter 3 of the **Bhagavad Gita**, known as **Karma Yoga**, is a profound discourse on the **importance of selfless action**. After explaining the philosophy of the eternal soul in Chapter 2, Krishna now clarifies **the role of action (Karma) in spiritual evolution**. Arjuna, still confused, asks Krishna why He is encouraging him to fight if **knowledge (Jnana)** is superior to action. In response, Krishna emphasizes that **action is essential and unavoidable** in the material world, and renouncing action is not the path to liberation.

Krishna explains the **principle of Karma Yoga—selfless action performed without attachment to results**. He teaches that every individual is bound by their inherent nature (**Swabhava**) and **must act according to their prescribed duties (Dharma)**. He warns against **inaction (Sanyasa)**, explaining that even a wise person must engage in duty for the welfare of society. Krishna uses the **example of great leaders** who perform their responsibilities selflessly, inspiring others to do the same.

He introduces the concept of **Yajna (sacrifice)**, explaining that all actions should be offered as a sacred duty to the divine. Actions performed with selfish motives bind an individual to the cycle of birth and rebirth, whereas those performed with devotion and detachment lead to liberation (**Moksha**). Krishna stresses that one should act **without ego and personal desire**, dedicating all actions to the higher purpose of sustaining harmony in the universe.

Krishna also warns against **desires and attachments**, which create obstacles in the path of righteousness. He explains the influence of the **three Gunas (Sattva, Rajas, and Tamas)** on human behavior and urges Arjuna to transcend them by surrendering to **pure, selfless action**. He advises Arjuna to **control the senses**, cultivate self-discipline, and perform his duty with devotion.

The chapter concludes with a call to action, where Krishna urges Arjuna to rise above confusion, surrender to divine will, and fight with **detachment and faith**. **Karma Yoga teaches that by performing selfless actions in a spirit of devotion and renunciation, one attains true freedom and inner peace.**

Chapter 4: Jnana Karma Sanyasa Yoga (The Yoga of Knowledge and Renunciation of Action)

Chapter 4 of the **Bhagavad Gita**, known as **Jnana Karma Sanyasa Yoga**, elaborates on the relationship between **knowledge (Jnana), action (Karma), and renunciation (Sanyasa)**. Krishna explains that **true renunciation is not the abandonment of action but the renunciation of ego and attachment to results**. He further deepens Arjuna's understanding of Karma Yoga by introducing **divine wisdom (Jnana)** and explaining how selfless action, performed with knowledge, leads to liberation.

Krishna begins by revealing that **the wisdom of the Gita is eternal** and was first taught by Him to **Vivasvan (the Sun God), who passed it on to Manu and the great sages**. Arjuna is astonished and questions how Krishna, born in a human form, could have given this knowledge in the past. Krishna then reveals His **divine nature**, explaining that He is **unborn, eternal, and manifests Himself whenever Dharma declines and Adharma rises**. He proclaims:

"Whenever there is a decline in righteousness and a rise in unrighteousness, I manifest Myself to protect the virtuous, destroy the wicked, and re-establish Dharma."

This declaration establishes Krishna's role as the **Supreme Divine Being (Ishvara)**, emphasizing that He incarnates in different ages to guide humanity.

Krishna then explains the **importance of performing action with knowledge**. Actions performed with ignorance bind one to the cycle of birth and rebirth **(Samsara)**, whereas those performed with wisdom and devotion lead to **liberation (Moksha)**. He clarifies that **Karma Yoga, when combined with Jnana (spiritual knowledge), leads to true renunciation**—one continues to act in the world but remains **unattached to the fruits of action**.

He introduces the concept of **sacrificial action (Yajna)**, explaining that all actions should be performed as offerings to the divine. He describes different forms of sacrifice, including:

- **Sacrifice of material possessions**
- **Sacrifice of knowledge**
- **Sacrifice of self-discipline and meditation**

Krishna emphasizes that **knowledge (Jnana) is the highest form of sacrifice**, as it destroys ignorance and reveals the ultimate truth. He encourages Arjuna to seek wisdom from realized sages, explaining that **true knowledge leads to freedom from doubts and attachment**. He assures Arjuna that even the greatest sinner can cross the ocean of suffering through the **fire of knowledge**.

The chapter concludes with Krishna urging Arjuna to **rise with faith, destroy doubts with the sword of knowledge, and act with wisdom and devotion. Jnana Karma Sanyasa Yoga teaches that the combination of knowledge, action, and renunciation leads to spiritual liberation, making it one of the most profound teachings of the Bhagavad Gita.**

Chapter 5: Karma Sanyasa Yoga (The Yoga of Renunciation)

In **Chapter 5 of the Bhagavad Gita, Karma Sanyasa Yoga**, Krishna explains the relationship between **renunciation (Sanyasa) and selfless action (Karma Yoga)**. Arjuna is confused about which path is superior—**renouncing all action or performing selfless action**

without attachment. Krishna clarifies that **both renunciation and selfless action lead to liberation**, but **Karma Yoga (selfless action) is the superior path** because it allows one to remain engaged in the world while attaining spiritual realization.

Krishna explains that **true renunciation is not about abandoning all actions but renouncing attachment to the fruits of action**. A true renunciate is one who acts without selfish motives and remains unaffected by success or failure. Those who perform **Karma Yoga with wisdom** and surrender to God attain **inner peace and liberation (Moksha)** while continuing their worldly duties.

He then describes the **qualities of a realized person** (Jnani), explaining that such a person:

- Sees **no difference between a learned Brahmin, a cow, an elephant, a dog, or an outcaste**—as they recognize the divine essence in all beings (**Samatvam, or equanimity**).
- Is **detached from worldly pleasures and sorrows**, unaffected by pain or joy.
- Finds **true happiness within (Atmananda)** rather than seeking it externally.

Krishna emphasizes that those who are free from **desires, attachments, and ego** attain **eternal peace and union with the divine**. He describes the **state of a liberated soul (Jivanmukta)**, who remains engaged in action but is internally detached, much like a lotus leaf that remains untouched by water. Such a person **acts selflessly,**

offering all actions to God, thus breaking free from the cycle of birth and death (**Samsara**).

A key teaching of this chapter is **the concept of the "city of nine gates"**, referring to the human body. Krishna explains that the **self-realized person understands that the body is merely a dwelling place for the soul** and remains **detached from bodily experiences**, knowing that the true self is beyond the physical form.

Krishna concludes by highlighting **the path to supreme bliss**—one must:

- **Control the senses and mind** through meditation and self-discipline.
- **Surrender all actions to the divine** with devotion.
- **See the unity in all beings** and cultivate universal love and compassion.

Ultimately, **Karma Sanyasa Yoga teaches that renunciation does not mean abandoning life but surrendering the ego and attachments**. By practicing **selfless action with wisdom and devotion**, one attains **inner peace, spiritual enlightenment, and liberation (Moksha)**. Krishna assures Arjuna that a person who follows this path **will merge with the Supreme Brahman (Divine Consciousness), experiencing eternal joy and freedom.**

Chapter 6: Dhyana Yoga (The Yoga of Meditation)

In **Chapter 6 of the Bhagavad Gita, Dhyana Yoga,** Krishna expounds on the significance of **meditation (Dhyana) as a means of spiritual realization and self-**

mastery. He explains how meditation enables a seeker to transcend worldly distractions, attain inner peace, and ultimately unite with the Divine. This chapter is one of the most profound teachings on the **practice of meditation (Raja Yoga)** and the qualities of a true yogi.

Krishna begins by explaining the qualities of a **true renunciate (Sanyasi) and yogi**. He clarifies that **mere physical renunciation of worldly life does not make one a true Sanyasi**; instead, one who performs duties selflessly and without attachment is a true renunciate. A yogi is superior to ascetics, scholars, and ritualists because they are engaged in **meditative absorption (Samadhi)** and **devotion to the Supreme**.

He then describes the **path of meditation** as a means to self-realization:

- A yogi should **practice meditation in seclusion, in a clean and sacred place**, free from distractions.

- The **posture** of meditation is crucial: one should sit firmly, keeping the back, neck, and head aligned, focusing the mind on the divine.

- The **breath should be regulated**, and the senses withdrawn from external temptations to achieve inner stillness.

- **The mind should be one-pointedly fixed on the self (Atman) or the divine (Krishna)** without wavering.

Krishna emphasizes the importance of **self-discipline (Abhyasa) and detachment (Vairagya)** in meditation. He warns that the mind is restless and difficult to control, but with **constant practice and perseverance**, a yogi can achieve inner tranquility. He assures Arjuna that **even if one fails in meditation in this life, their efforts are never wasted**—they will be born in favorable circumstances in the next life and continue their spiritual progress.

One of the most profound teachings in this chapter is Krishna's declaration that **a devoted yogi is the highest among all seekers**. Among different types of spiritual aspirants, a **Bhakti Yogi (one devoted to God with love and surrender) is the most exalted**. He proclaims:

"Among all yogis, the one who worships Me with faith, and whose inner self is merged in Me, is the most supreme."

Krishna describes the **state of an enlightened yogi**, who:

- Is **free from desires, attachments, and ego.**

- **Sees all beings as equal** and treats friends, enemies, and strangers with impartiality.

- **Remains undisturbed by worldly pleasures and sorrows**, experiencing divine bliss within.

Ultimately, **Dhyana Yoga teaches that through meditation, self-discipline, and devotion, one can attain self-realization and merge with the Divine.** Krishna assures Arjuna that **meditation leads to liberation (Moksha) and eternal peace**, making it a powerful spiritual practice for those seeking enlightenment.

Chapter 7: Jnana Vijnana Yoga (The Yoga of Knowledge and Wisdom)

In **Chapter 7 of the Bhagavad Gita, Jnana Vijnana Yoga**, Krishna expounds on the **nature of divine knowledge (Jnana) and transcendental wisdom (Vijnana)**. This chapter reveals the **ultimate reality of God, the material and spiritual worlds, and the different types of devotees** who seek Him. It serves as a bridge between theoretical knowledge and experiential realization.

Krishna begins by encouraging Arjuna to listen attentively, as He is about to reveal **supreme wisdom** that will free him from all worldly illusions. He emphasizes that among thousands of seekers, only a rare few strive for true self-realization, and even among them, only a handful truly understand Him in full.

Krishna explains His **twofold nature—the material (Prakriti) and spiritual (Purusha)** aspects of existence. The **material world (Apara Prakriti)** consists of **eight elements—earth, water, fire, air, space, mind, intellect, and ego—**which form the basis of the physical universe. However, beyond this is **Para Prakriti (the higher, divine energy)**, which is the **eternal consciousness that sustains all life**. This higher energy is Krishna Himself, the **Supreme Being who pervades and governs everything**.

Krishna asserts that He is the **ultimate cause of all existence**, the origin and dissolution of the universe. Everything arises from Him, and nothing is beyond His divine will. Despite being present in all things, He remains **unaffected by material nature (Maya)**. However, **due to Maya's illusion, people fail to recognize His divine presence**. Maya binds individuals to the material world, making it difficult for them to perceive the Supreme Truth.

Krishna categorizes devotees into **four types**, based on their motivations:

1. **The distressed (Aarta)** – Those who seek God in times of suffering.

2. **The seekers of wealth (Artharthi)** – Those who worship for material gain.

3. **The inquisitive (Jijnasu)** – Those who seek spiritual knowledge.

4. **The wise (Jnani)** – Those who truly understand and love God unconditionally.

Among these, Krishna declares that the **Jnani (the wise one who worships with unwavering devotion) is the dearest to Him** because such a soul seeks Him alone, without any selfish desires. This **selfless devotion (Bhakti) leads to liberation (Moksha)**.

Krishna also explains the **varied ways in which people worship different deities**, believing that these deities fulfill their desires. However, He clarifies that all such worship ultimately reaches Him, as He is the source of all divine manifestations. Yet, those who worship with material motives remain bound to the cycle of birth and death. Only those who surrender to Krishna with **pure devotion** attain eternal liberation.

The chapter concludes with Krishna stating that **true wisdom lies in knowing Him as the Supreme Reality**, beyond all illusions of the world. Those who take refuge in Him, transcending material desires, attain **eternal peace and spiritual fulfillment**.

Chapter 8: Akshara Brahma Yoga (The Yoga of the Imperishable Absolute)

In **Chapter 8: Akshara Brahma Yoga** of the Bhagavad Gita, Krishna explains the **nature of the imperishable Brahman (Akshara), the ultimate goal of life, and the process of attaining liberation (Moksha)**. Arjuna, eager to understand profound spiritual truths, asks Krishna about **Brahman (the Supreme Reality), Adhyatma (the individual self), Karma (action), Adhibhuta (the material world), Adhidaiva (the divine governing forces), and Adhiyajna (the Supreme Lord present in sacrifices)**. Krishna responds by describing **Brahman as the eternal, unchanging reality beyond the physical world, while Adhyatma refers to the individual soul (Atman) residing in the body. Karma encompasses all actions that lead to rebirth, Adhibhuta represents perishable material existence, Adhidaiva signifies the cosmic intelligence governing creation, and Adhiyajna is Krishna Himself, residing in the heart of all beings as the divine witness.** Krishna then reveals the **importance of remembering Him at the time of death,** stating that **one's final thoughts determine their next birth**. He advises that **those who fix their mind on Him at the moment of death, with unwavering devotion, attain the eternal abode and do not return to the cycle of birth and death**. He describes the process of **yogic meditation (Bhakti Yoga and Dhyana Yoga), wherein a seeker withdraws their senses, focuses their consciousness on the center of the forehead (Ajna Chakra), and chants the sacred syllable "Om" while thinking of Krishna**—this ensures **direct liberation to His divine realm (Param Dham)**. Krishna contrasts the **two cosmic paths** that souls take after death—the **path of light (Shukla Gati), leading to liberation, and the path of darkness (Krishna Gati), leading to rebirth**. He explains that **those who realize the Supreme and attain Krishna do not return to the material world, while those who follow material desires remain bound by the cycle of life and death**. This chapter highlights the **importance of unwavering devotion (Bhakti), constant remembrance of Krishna, and spiritual discipline in attaining liberation**, emphasizing that **knowing and surrendering to the Supreme Consciousness is the only way to transcend mortality and attain eternal bliss in the divine realm.**

Chapter 9: Raja Vidya Raja Guhya Yoga (The Yoga of Royal Knowledge and Royal Secret)

In **Chapter 9: Raja Vidya Raja Guhya Yoga** of the Bhagavad Gita, Krishna reveals the **most profound and confidential knowledge**—the supreme wisdom that leads to liberation. This chapter is called the "Yoga of Royal Knowledge and Royal Secret" because it unveils the highest spiritual truth, known only to those with **unwavering faith and devotion**. Krishna declares that **this knowledge is the king of sciences (Raja Vidya), the greatest secret (Raja Guhya), supremely purifying, and directly realizable**. He explains that **those who lack faith in the divine truth remain bound to the cycle of birth and death, failing to attain liberation**. Krishna emphasizes that **He is the ultimate reality and the cause of all creation, pervading the universe as an imperishable, formless, and eternal presence.** He describes how **He supports the entire cosmos, yet remains detached from it, similar to how the wind moves within space without being bound to it.** Although **He appears to be within the world, He transcends it, existing beyond material nature (Prakriti).** Krishna further explains the **cyclic nature of creation and dissolution**, stating that **all beings arise from His divine will and merge back into Him at the end of cosmic time (Kalpa).** He governs the **laws of nature, yet remains uninvolved in individual karma, allowing beings to act according to their free will.** He then speaks about **the power of devotion (Bhakti Yoga), asserting that those who worship Him with love, even if imperfect, will surely attain liberation.** Krishna reassures that **even the most sinful individuals can become virtuous if they surrender to Him with sincerity.** He expresses His **equal love for all beings**, yet grants special grace to those who offer **pure devotion**. He highlights that **simple offering such as a leaf, flower, fruit, or water, given with love, are accepted by Him**, proving that **sincere devotion is more valuable than elaborate rituals.** Krishna also explains that **devotees** who engage in constant remembrance of Him, dedicating all their actions to Him, are protected and guided by Him. He declares that **anyone—regardless of their background, gender, or past actions—can attain the supreme goal through devotion.** He advises Arjuna to **always think of Him, worship Him, and surrender fully, ensuring liberation from the material cycle of existence.** The essence of this chapter is that **faith, love, and surrender to Krishna lead to eternal bliss and freedom from all suffering.** Thus, **Raja Vidya Raja Guhya Yoga** emphasizes that **pure devotion (Bhakti) is the highest path to realizing the Supreme Being, surpassing all other forms of spiritual practices.**

Chapter 10: Vibhuti Yoga (The Yoga of Divine Glories)

In **Chapter 10: Vibhuti Yoga (The Yoga of Divine Glories)**, Krishna reveals to Arjuna the **infinite manifestations of His divine power** that pervade the universe. He explains that **He is the ultimate source of all creation, the supreme cause of everything, and the essence of all that is magnificent, powerful, and virtuous.** Krishna declares that **His divine glories (Vibhutis) are present in every aspect of existence—both animate and inanimate—and that the entire cosmos operates under His divine will.** He begins by explaining that **the wise who realize His supreme nature attain unwavering devotion and knowledge,** freeing themselves from delusion. He describes that **those with purified hearts, constantly meditating on Him, receive divine wisdom, which dispels ignorance and leads them to liberation.** Krishna then reveals that **He is** the original creator of all beings, including sages, gods, and celestial beings, and that **His presence is eternal and beyond human comprehension**. Arjuna, overwhelmed by Krishna's divine revelations, expresses deep gratitude and devotion, acknowledging Krishna as **the Supreme Lord, the eternal truth, and the source of all wisdom**. Arjuna humbly requests Krishna to elaborate on **His divine manifestations**, so he may understand and appreciate them further. In response, Krishna enumerates **His supreme manifestations in various aspects of the world**—stating that **among the Adityas (solar deities), He is Vishnu; among the luminaries, He is the radiant Sun; among the Maruts (wind gods), He is Marichi; among stars, He is the Moon**. He further declares, **"Among the Vedas, I am the Sama Veda; among deities, I am Indra; among senses, I am the mind; among living beings, I am consciousness."** Krishna continues listing His glories, saying, **"I am the power of the strong, the wisdom of the wise, the silence of the seekers, and the righteousness of the virtuous."** He emphasizes that **His divine essence is present in the greatest and most extraordinary forms across nature, knowledge, strength, and spirituality**. He explains that **He is the source of everything beautiful and powerful, including great warriors, sages, and celestial beings such as Brihaspati, Skanda, and Kubera**. Krishna also declares, **"Among mountains, I am the Himalayas; among rivers, I am the Ganges; among trees, I am the sacred Peepal tree; among animals, I am the lion; among birds, I am Garuda."** Through these revelations, Krishna conveys that **whenever one sees something extraordinary, powerful, or divine, it is a reflection of**

His supreme existence. He concludes by stating that **His glories are limitless, and what He has described is only a fraction of His divine manifestations**. Finally, Krishna tells Arjuna that **He alone sustains the entire universe with just a fraction of His infinite being, reinforcing that He is the supreme force governing all of creation**. This chapter emphasizes **the omnipresence of the Divine, encouraging devotion, humility, and reverence for the Lord in every aspect of existence**.

Chapter 11: Vishvarupa Darshana Yoga (The Yoga of the Vision of the Universal Form)

In **Chapter 11: Vishvarupa Darshana Yoga (The Yoga of the Vision of the Universal Form)**, Krishna grants Arjuna a divine vision to perceive His **cosmic, all-encompassing form**—a moment that becomes the most awe-inspiring revelation of the Bhagavad Gita. After hearing about Krishna's divine glories in the previous chapter, Arjuna expresses his deep faith and devotion, yet he yearns for **a direct experience of Krishna's supreme, universal form**. Understanding Arjuna's desire, Krishna blesses him with **divine eyes**, enabling him to witness the **Vishvarupa**, a form that cannot be seen with ordinary human perception. As Krishna manifests His **cosmic form**, Arjuna sees an **infinite, resplendent being with countless faces, eyes, and arms, stretching across the entire universe**. The form is adorned with **divine ornaments, wielding celestial weapons, and radiating the brilliance of a thousand suns**. Within Krishna's universal body, Arjuna perceives **all beings—gods, sages, celestial beings, and mortal creatures—existing within Him**, symbolizing that Krishna is the ultimate source and sustainer of all life. He also witnesses **the entire cosmic order, past, present, and future, unfolding within this supreme form**. As Arjuna gazes in awe, he sees **the terrifying aspect of Krishna's form**, with **fiery mouths consuming countless warriors, including Duryodhana and other Kauravas**, signifying the inevitable destruction in the great war. Arjuna realizes that Krishna is not just the divine protector but also **the all-powerful force of time (Kala), which ensures the cycle of creation and destruction**. Shaken by this overwhelming vision, Arjuna trembles with **both devotion and fear**, realizing that everything is predestined by Krishna's will. He acknowledges Krishna as **the supreme being, beyond all gods and sages, the eternal, imperishable reality that governs the cosmos**. In deep reverence, Arjuna **bows in surrender**, seeking forgiveness for any unintended offenses he may have committed in ignorance. Overwhelmed, he requests Krishna to return to His **gentler, human-like form**, as the Vishvarupa is too immense and fearsome for him to bear. Krishna, in His boundless compassion, **reassures Arjuna and resumes His familiar form**, comforting him and reminding him that **only through unwavering devotion, surrender, and selfless love can one truly understand and attain Him**. This chapter serves as a powerful reminder that **Krishna is the supreme, omnipresent force guiding the universe**, reinforcing the themes of **divine omnipotence, destiny, and surrender to the Lord's will**. Through this vision, Arjuna gains clarity about his duty in the war, understanding that he is merely an instrument in Krishna's grand cosmic plan. **Vishvarupa Darshana Yoga teaches that true wisdom** comes from recognizing the divine in all aspects of existence and surrendering to the higher cosmic order.

Chapter 12: Bhakti Yoga (The Yoga of Devotion)

In **Chapter 12: Bhakti Yoga (The Yoga of Devotion)**, Krishna extols **devotion (bhakti)** as the highest and easiest path to attaining Him, emphasizing **love, faith, and surrender** over intellectual knowledge or rigorous asceticism. At the beginning of the chapter, Arjuna, having witnessed Krishna's **cosmic form (Vishvarupa)**, asks whether **worshiping a formless, unmanifested Brahman (Nirguna Brahman) or a personal, embodied God (Saguna Brahman) is superior**. Krishna explains that while both paths can lead to liberation, **worshiping the personal form of God with love and devotion is easier and more accessible** for the common seeker. Devotion fosters **a deep, emotional connection with the Divine**, while focusing on the formless absolute requires intense discipline, detachment, and intellectual abstraction, which is difficult for most people.

Krishna assures that **He personally takes care of His devoted followers**, guiding them toward liberation, provided they **surrender completely and act with unwavering faith**. He describes the **qualities of an ideal devotee (bhakta)**, emphasizing that a true devotee is **free from malice, humble, content, self-controlled, and compassionate**, treating friends and foes alike and remaining **detached from material possessions and ego-driven desires**. Such a devotee **neither rejoices nor despairs, neither craves nor resents, and remains**

peaceful in all circumstances, relying entirely on Krishna's grace.

Furthermore, Krishna offers **multiple approaches to devotion**, making Bhakti Yoga inclusive for seekers of all levels. The highest path is **total absorption in Krishna through unwavering devotion**. If that is too difficult, He suggests **constant remembrance of Him through practice**. If even that is not feasible, one can engage in **selfless service (karma yoga), performing duties as an offering to Krishna**, which eventually purifies the mind and leads to devotion. Lastly, for those unable to practice any of these methods, Krishna advises cultivating **detachment and surrendering the results of all actions to Him**.

The essence of **Bhakti Yoga** is that **devotion is not restricted by caste, knowledge, or renunciation but is open to all, regardless of background or ability**. Unlike Jnana Yoga (path of knowledge) or Karma Yoga (path of action), which require deep philosophical insight or rigorous self-discipline, **Bhakti Yoga simply requires love and surrender**. Krishna reassures Arjuna that **His devotees will never perish**, as He personally uplifts and protects them. **Through faith, humility, and love, one can attain divine grace effortlessly.**

This chapter is **a beacon of hope and inclusivity**, emphasizing that **God does not demand elaborate rituals or intellectual brilliance—He seeks only pure, selfless love.** Krishna's promise that **He is easily attainable through devotion** makes Bhakti Yoga the most **approachable and emotionally fulfilling path to**

spiritual enlightenment. This chapter has had a profound influence on Hindu spirituality, inspiring numerous **Bhakti movements**, saints, and poets across history. In conclusion, **Bhakti Yoga teaches that ultimate liberation (moksha) is not a distant goal but a heartfelt connection with the Divine, nurtured through unwavering love, faith, and selfless surrender.**

Chapter 13: Ksetra Ksetrajna Vibhaga Yoga (The Yoga of the Field and the Knower of the Field)

In **Chapter 13: Kṣetra-Kṣetrajña Vibhāga Yoga (The Yoga of the Field and the Knower of the Field)**, Krishna explains the **distinction between the physical body (Kṣetra) and the conscious self (Kṣetrajña)**, providing deep insights into the **nature of existence, self-realization, and the ultimate truth**. This chapter bridges **metaphysics and spiritual wisdom**, guiding seekers to discern the difference between the **material world and the eternal soul**.

Krishna begins by describing the **body as the "field" (Kṣetra)**—a temporary, changing entity composed of **the five elements (earth, water, fire, air, space), mind, intellect, and ego**. Just as a farmer cultivates a field, experiences in life shape and influence the body. However, **the true self, the "knower of the field" (Kṣetrajña), is the eternal consciousness that witnesses all changes but remains untouched by them.** Krishna identifies Himself as the Supreme Knower present in **all fields (bodies), emphasizing that divine consciousness pervades all beings**.

To understand this distinction, Krishna lists **the qualities (Jñāna or true knowledge) that lead to self-realization**. These include **humility, non-violence, patience, detachment from material possessions, inner purity, self-restraint, and devotion to God**. True knowledge is not just intellectual accumulation but the **cultivation of virtues that align the seeker with spiritual wisdom**. Krishna stresses that **real wisdom lies in recognizing the eternal soul within, beyond physical identity and worldly attachments**.

The **material world (Prakṛti) and the conscious self (Puruṣa)** are also discussed in this chapter. Prakṛti is the dynamic, ever-changing force that manifests as **mind, body, and senses**, while Puruṣa is the **unchanging witness, the eternal soul**. Their interaction gives rise to human experience—**attachment to Prakṛti leads to suffering, whereas realizing the self as Puruṣa brings liberation (Moksha)**.

Krishna further elaborates on **the Supreme Brahman, the ultimate reality**, which is **beginningless, formless, and beyond all dualities**. It is neither **born nor destroyed**, and those who recognize this transcendental truth free themselves from the cycle of birth and death (Samsara).

To attain liberation, Krishna advises **seeing the Divine presence in all beings and remaining detached from sensory distractions**. The wise perceive **unity in diversity**, understanding that the **same consciousness exists in every living being**. By cultivating **detachment**,

self-discipline, and devotion, one transcends the material world and attains **self-realization**.

Ultimately, **this chapter serves as a profound meditation on the nature of the self, reality, and the path to liberation.** It emphasizes that **self-knowledge is the key to overcoming ignorance, and true wisdom comes from recognizing the eternal soul beyond the perishable body.** By following **a life of humility, devotion, and discernment**, one can **transcend material limitations and unite with the divine consciousness.** Thus, **Kṣetra-Kṣetrajña Vibhāga Yoga offers a philosophical roadmap to enlightenment, urging seekers to look beyond the external and realize their inner divinity.**

Chapter 14: Gunatraya Vibhaga Yoga (The Yoga of the Division of the Three Gunas)

Chapter 14: Guna-Traya Vibhaga Yoga (The Yoga of the Division of the Three Gunas) delves into the **three fundamental qualities (gunas) of material nature—Sattva (purity), Rajas (passion), and Tamas (ignorance)**—which govern human behavior, perception, and spiritual progress. Krishna explains that all beings in the material world are influenced by these three gunas, which arise from **Prakriti (nature)** and bind the soul to the cycle of birth and rebirth. The chapter serves as a **guide to understanding the forces that shape consciousness** and offers the path to transcendence beyond them.

Krishna begins by stating that **he is the ultimate source of creation**, and everything in the universe is sustained by **his divine energy (Brahman)**. However, **the material world operates under the influence of the three gunas, which shape human tendencies and determine one's spiritual evolution**. These gunas exist in different proportions in every individual, and their dominance affects thoughts, actions, and destiny.

1. **Sattva (Purity, Knowledge, Harmony):** Sattva is the **guna of wisdom, clarity, and balance**. It is associated with **light, knowledge, and righteousness**, leading to **inner peace and self-realization**. Those dominated by Sattva cultivate **compassion, discipline, and spiritual understanding**. However, even Sattva, despite being a superior quality, binds the soul through **attachment to happiness and knowledge**.

2. **Rajas (Passion, Desire, Activity):** Rajas is the **guna of ambition, restlessness, and attachment to action**. It fuels **desires, greed, and worldly pursuits**, causing individuals to remain entangled in **material pleasures and suffering**. People influenced by Rajas are often driven by **ego, competition, and an insatiable craving for success**, leading to **stress and frustration** when desires remain unfulfilled.

3. **Tamas (Ignorance, Inertia, Darkness):** Tamas is the **guna of laziness, ignorance, and delusion**. It clouds wisdom and leads to **procrastination, negligence, and self-destructive behaviors**. Those dominated by Tamas indulge in **excessive sleep, addiction, violence, and confusion**,

remaining trapped in cycles of suffering without seeking higher knowledge.

Krishna explains that at the time of death, the **dominant guna** in an individual determines their next birth. A person with **Sattvic tendencies attains higher realms of existence**, a **Rajasic person is reborn into a life of struggle and desire**, while a **Tamasic individual descends into lower states of consciousness**.

However, Krishna assures that **one can transcend the gunas by cultivating detachment and devotion**. By surrendering to God and practicing selfless action (Karma Yoga), meditation (Dhyana Yoga), and spiritual knowledge (Jnana Yoga), one can rise above the influence of the gunas and attain liberation (Moksha).

Ultimately, **this chapter serves as a roadmap for self-improvement, guiding individuals to recognize their dominant guna and cultivate Sattva while striving to go beyond all gunas through devotion and self-realization**. Krishna encourages seekers to **become "Guna-atita" (beyond the gunas), free from material bondage, and united with the eternal divine consciousness**.

Chapter 15: Purushottama Yoga (The Yoga of the Supreme Person)

Chapter 15: Purushottama Yoga (The Yoga of the Supreme Person) explores the **eternal and perishable aspects of existence**, presenting a **philosophical understanding** of the Supreme Reality

(Purushottama). Krishna describes the **nature of the material world, the imperishable soul, and the ultimate goal of human life—liberation through devotion to the Supreme Person.** This chapter provides **a profound vision of reality**, helping seekers transcend material limitations and attain spiritual enlightenment.

Krishna begins by introducing the **metaphor of the Ashvattha tree (sacred fig tree)** with **roots above and branches below**, symbolizing the **illusory material world (Maya)**. The branches represent **various aspects of existence—human experiences, emotions, and actions**, while the roots signify **the divine source that nourishes life**. This **upside-down tree represents attachment to worldly desires**, which binds souls to the cycle of birth and death (Samsara). Krishna advises **cutting down this tree with the weapon of detachment and seeking the eternal, imperishable truth beyond material existence.**

Krishna then explains the **two types of beings in the universe—Kshara (perishable) and Akshara (imperishable). Kshara** refers to **all living beings who undergo birth and death**, bound by karma and material existence. **Akshara** represents the **eternal soul (Atman), which remains unchanged despite the body's transformation.** However, beyond both Kshara and Akshara is **Purushottama, the Supreme Person (Krishna himself), who transcends all limitations and sustains the entire universe.** By realizing and surrendering to Purushottama, one attains **freedom from ignorance and achieves Moksha (liberation).**

Krishna explains that the **individual soul (Jiva) is an eternal fragment of the Supreme**, but when it enters the material world, it becomes conditioned by **desires and sensory attachments**. Just as the wind carries fragrances, the soul carries **impressions from past lives**, leading to new births and experiences. However, **those with wisdom recognize this truth and strive for spiritual realization.**

Further, Krishna describes **his divine presence in all aspects of creation**—he is the **light of the sun and moon, the intelligence in humans, the strength of the strong, and the sacred syllable "Om" in the Vedas**. He states that **those who remain ignorant of his supreme nature remain trapped in illusion**, while those who recognize him as **Purushottama break free from the bondage of life and death**.

Krishna concludes that **only through unwavering devotion (Bhakti) can one truly understand and attain the Supreme Person**. He urges Arjuna and all seekers to **transcend material dualities and realize the eternal connection with the Divine**. By recognizing Krishna as **the ultimate refuge and surrendering to him with a pure heart**, one attains **eternal peace and liberation from worldly suffering**.

Thus, **Chapter 15 serves as a spiritual guide, teaching seekers to detach from the transient material world, recognize the Supreme Person, and attain divine union through devotion and wisdom**. It provides a **clear vision of reality, emphasizing the imperishable nature** of the soul and the supreme goal of life—liberation in the presence of Purushottama.

Chapter 16: Daivasura Sampad Vibhaga Yoga (The Yoga of the Divine and the Demonic Qualities)

Chapter 16: Daivasura Sampad Vibhaga Yoga (The Yoga of the Divine and the Demonic Qualities) explores the **two fundamental tendencies within human nature—divine (Daivi) and demonic (Asuri)—** which determine an individual's spiritual progress or downfall. Krishna explains that those who cultivate **divine qualities attain liberation (Moksha), while those with demonic tendencies remain trapped in the cycle of birth and death (Samsara).** This chapter serves as a **moral and ethical guide**, urging seekers to embrace righteousness and reject destructive qualities.

Krishna begins by listing **divine qualities (Daivi Sampad)** that lead to spiritual elevation. These include **fearlessness, truthfulness, self-restraint, compassion, humility, purity of heart, non-violence (Ahimsa), detachment, forgiveness, devotion to God, and self-discipline.** Such virtues align individuals with **Dharma (righteousness), fostering inner peace and ultimate liberation.** Those who embody these qualities live in harmony with themselves and the world, experiencing **spiritual growth and enlightenment.**

In contrast, Krishna describes **demonic qualities (Asuri Sampad)** that lead to downfall and suffering. These include **hypocrisy, arrogance, harshness, anger, cruelty, ignorance, selfish desires, lack of self-control, and disregard for moral principles.** Individuals who exhibit these tendencies act **driven by ego and materialistic pursuits, disregarding divine law and ethical responsibilities.** They remain **trapped in delusion, constantly seeking worldly pleasures without concern for their spiritual well-being.**

Krishna explains that those with demonic tendencies **reject the concept of a higher order and believe the world is purely materialistic, without divine presence or purpose.** They become **obsessed with fulfilling selfish desires, accumulating wealth, and exerting dominance over others.** Their unchecked greed and pride **lead them to unethical actions, resulting in further bondage to Samsara (cycle of rebirth).**

Further, Krishna warns that **such individuals ignore scriptures and moral values**, considering themselves supreme and invincible. Their attachment to **lust, anger, and arrogance** blinds them, making them incapable of distinguishing right from wrong. Their fate is **spiritual ruin, as they descend into lower states of existence (Tamas) due to their misguided actions and ignorance.**

Krishna emphasizes that **one's destiny is determined by the qualities one nurtures.** Those who **embrace divine virtues** progress toward **self-realization and divine union**, while those who indulge in demonic tendencies face **spiritual regression.** However, **free will exists**, and individuals can consciously choose **the path of righteousness (Dharma) over darkness.**

In conclusion, **Chapter 16 provides a blueprint for ethical and spiritual living,** highlighting the **importance of cultivating divine virtues while**

rejecting negative tendencies. Krishna urges Arjuna—and all seekers—to **adopt righteousness, follow scriptural guidance, and surrender to divine wisdom.** By **choosing the path of virtue and devotion**, one can attain **inner peace, spiritual liberation, and eternal bliss in the presence of the Divine.**

Chapter 17: Sraddhatraya Vibhaga Yoga (The Yoga of Threefold Faith)

Chapter 17: Sraddhatraya Vibhaga Yoga (The Yoga of Threefold Faith) explores the **different types of faith (Shraddha)** and how they influence an individual's actions, thoughts, and spiritual growth. Krishna explains that faith is inherent in every human being, but its nature varies based on one's inner disposition, which is governed by the **three Gunas (modes of material nature): Sattva (goodness), Rajas (passion), and Tamas (ignorance).** The chapter emphasizes that **faith shapes an individual's character, determines their destiny, and influences their journey toward liberation or bondage.**

Krishna begins by stating that a person's **faith aligns with their inherent nature (Svabhava)** and that this faith dictates their **beliefs, worship, and actions.** Those dominated by **Sattva Guna** exhibit **pure, sincere, and noble faith.** They worship **divine beings and seek knowledge, truth, and self-discipline.** Their actions are motivated by **selflessness and righteousness**, leading them toward **spiritual enlightenment and ultimate liberation (Moksha).**

In contrast, individuals influenced by **Rajas Guna** possess **faith driven by material desires, ambition, and**

attachment. They worship **powerful and ambitious deities, seeking wealth, success, and personal gratification.** Their actions, though energetic, are often **self-centered and ego-driven, leading to temporary worldly gains but not lasting spiritual fulfillment.**

Those under the dominance of **Tamas Guna** exhibit **blind faith, ignorance, and destructive tendencies.** They engage in **superstitious or harmful rituals and worship lower entities such as spirits or dark forces.** Their actions are often **violent, deluded, and devoid of ethical consideration, leading to spiritual degradation.** Krishna warns that such individuals remain **trapped in darkness, unable to progress toward higher consciousness.**

Krishna further explains that the **type of food one consumes also reflects their nature and influences their spiritual state.**

- **Sattvic food** (pure, fresh, nutritious, and moderate) promotes **clarity, longevity, and spiritual awareness.**

- **Rajasic food** (spicy, bitter, excessively hot, or stimulating) fuels **restlessness, aggression, and desires.**

- **Tamasic food** (stale, impure, excessive, or intoxicating) leads to **laziness, delusion, and ignorance.**

Similarly, Krishna categorizes **sacrifices (Yajnas), austerities (Tapas), and charity (Dana)** based on the three Gunas.

- **Sattvic sacrifices, austerities, and charity** are performed **selflessly, with devotion and without expectation of rewards.**

- **Rajasic actions** are motivated by **ego, personal gain, and societal recognition.**

- **Tamasic practices** are performed **without faith, understanding, or adherence to spiritual principles.**

In conclusion, **Krishna emphasizes that faith is the foundation of human existence**, influencing every aspect of life. To attain **spiritual progress and liberation, one must cultivate Sattvic faith**, engage in **pure actions**, and align their life with **divine principles**. By practicing **selfless devotion, righteous living, and inner discipline**, individuals can **transcend worldly bondage and realize their true spiritual nature.**

Chapter 18: Moksha Sanyasa Yoga (The Yoga of Liberation and Renunciation)

Chapter 18: Moksha Sanyasa Yoga (The Yoga of Liberation and Renunciation) serves as the grand conclusion of the **Bhagavad Gita**, summarizing its key teachings and guiding Arjuna toward the path of **self-realization, duty, and ultimate liberation (Moksha).** In this chapter, Krishna explains the **true meaning of renunciation (Sanyasa)** and how it differs from **mere abandonment of actions.** He clarifies that renunciation does not mean **escaping responsibilities but performing one's duty without attachment to results.**

Krishna begins by distinguishing between **Sanyasa (renunciation of desire-driven actions)** and **Tyaga (selfless renunciation of attachment to actions)**. While some believe that **giving up all actions leads to liberation,** Krishna states that essential duties, especially those aligned with righteousness (Dharma), must never be abandoned. True renunciation lies in **detaching from the fruits of action, rather than avoiding action itself.**

He then classifies **action (Karma) based on the three Gunas (modes of nature):**

- **Sattvic action** is performed **selflessly, without desire for personal gain, and in harmony with Dharma.** It leads to **purity, wisdom, and spiritual progress.**

- **Rajasic action** is driven by **ego, ambition, and attachment to success or failure.** It results in **bondage and repeated cycles of birth and death.**

- **Tamasic action** is performed **without understanding, purpose, or moral consideration.** It is rooted in **ignorance, negligence, and destructiveness.**

Krishna further explains the **five factors that determine the outcome of any action: the body, the doer, the senses, the mind/intellect, and divine will (the ultimate controller).** He emphasizes that **one should act without ego,** recognizing that all actions are governed by these factors, and true wisdom lies in **seeing oneself as merely an instrument of the Divine.**

He then describes the **three types of knowledge, action, and the doer:**

- **Sattvic knowledge** sees the **one eternal reality (Brahman) in all beings,** leading to **unity and wisdom.**

- **Rajasic knowledge** perceives **diversity and separateness,** causing **confusion and attachment.**

- **Tamasic knowledge** is **deluded, narrow-minded, and disconnected from truth.**

Krishna also explains **the duties (Swadharma) associated with different castes (Varna) and temperaments.** He emphasizes that **performing one's duty with devotion, without selfish motives, leads to perfection and liberation.** Even imperfectly performed **personal duty (Swadharma) is superior to excelling in another's duty (Paradharma).**

Krishna then reveals **the ultimate path to liberation: complete surrender to the Divine (Bhakti).** He declares that those who **abandon all desires, ego, and doubts, and take refuge in Him with faith, will attain Moksha (eternal freedom).**

In his final message, Krishna urges Arjuna to **rise, fight, and fulfill his duty as a warrior (Kshatriya),** knowing that **he is merely an instrument of divine will.** Arjuna, now enlightened, overcomes his doubts and prepares for battle, signifying his acceptance of Krishna's wisdom.

Thus, **Chapter 18 concludes the Bhagavad Gita with a call to selfless action, faith, and surrender, guiding seekers toward the highest goal—liberation from the cycle of birth and death.**

Conclusion

The **Bhagavad Gita's 18 chapters provide a profound spiritual roadmap** for life, guiding individuals toward self-realization, righteousness, and divine wisdom. Its teachings remain timeless, applicable to all aspects of human existence, inspiring seekers on the path of truth and liberation.

3 The setting of the Kurukshetra battlefield

The **Bhagavad Gita**, one of the most revered scriptures in Hindu philosophy, is set against the backdrop of the **Kurukshetra battlefield**, where the great war of the **Mahabharata** takes place. This setting is not just a physical battlefield but also a metaphorical one, representing the conflict within the human mind and soul. The war signifies the struggle between **righteousness (Dharma) and unrighteousness (Adharma), duty and hesitation, knowledge and ignorance, action and inaction.**

Kurukshetra: The Sacred Land of Battle

Kurukshetra, known as the **"Dharmakshetra"** or the **"field of Dharma,"** is located in present-day Haryana, India. It was considered a **sacred land even before the Mahabharata war**, associated with many Vedic rituals and sacrifices. The battlefield was chosen not just for its strategic location but for its **spiritual significance**, as battles fought on this land were believed to be guided by divine forces and higher cosmic principles.

According to the **Mahabharata**, the Kurukshetra war was not just a political struggle but a war of cosmic importance, symbolizing the eternal fight between good and evil. The **Kauravas** (representing greed, ego, and unrighteousness) and the **Pandavas** (symbolizing truth, justice, and duty) assembled their armies on this sacred plain, preparing for a war that would determine the fate of the world.

The Armies and the Grand War Formation

The war at Kurukshetra was one of the largest and most destructive conflicts in Indian mythology. Both sides were prepared with vast armies, composed of great warriors, divine beings, and celestial weapons. The **Pandavas**, led by **Yudhishthira, Bhima, Arjuna, Nakula, and Sahadeva**, were supported by Lord **Krishna** as Arjuna's charioteer and guide. The **Kauravas**, led by **Duryodhana**, had formidable warriors like **Bhishma, Dronacharya, Karna, and Ashwatthama** on their side.

On the **first day of battle**, both armies stood facing each other in **military formations (Vyuhas)**. The Kauravas had a larger army, but the Pandavas had **Krishna's wisdom and divine support**. The conches were blown, and the air filled with the sounds of war drums and chants, marking the beginning of the great conflict.

Arjuna's Moral Dilemma and the Birth of the Bhagavad Gita

As both sides stood ready, **Arjuna**, the mightiest warrior among the Pandavas, was filled with **doubt and despair**. Looking at his own family, teachers, and loved ones in the enemy ranks, he **questioned the morality of war**. He saw revered elders like **Bhishma and Dronacharya**, who had once protected and nurtured him, standing as his opponents. This inner turmoil led to a profound existential crisis, making him **drop his bow (Gandiva) and refuse to fight.**

It is at this moment that **Krishna, his charioteer and divine guide, begins his discourse—the Bhagavad Gita.** Krishna addresses Arjuna's doubts, urging him to rise above personal emotions and act according to his **Dharma (duty).**

The Symbolism of the Battlefield

The battlefield of Kurukshetra represents **the inner battlefield of the mind**, where one constantly fights between right and wrong, action and inaction, faith and doubt. Krishna's teachings to Arjuna extend beyond war—they symbolize the **universal struggles faced by every human being in life.** The war itself becomes a **spiritual allegory**, where the true victory is not just over the enemy but over one's **own weaknesses, illusions, and fears.**

Divine Forces at Play

The Kurukshetra war was not just fought by mortal warriors but was also influenced by **divine and cosmic**

energies. Many celestial beings observed and participated in the war. The presence of Lord **Krishna**, who is an incarnation of **Vishnu**, signifies the intervention of the divine to restore Dharma. Krishna's role was unique—he did not wield any weapons but guided Arjuna toward self-realization and righteous action.

Moreover, the **Bhagavad Gita itself is considered a divine revelation**, where Krishna imparts the ultimate spiritual wisdom to Arjuna. This dialogue transforms Arjuna from a warrior in doubt to a **realized soul, ready to act without attachment.**

The Ultimate Decision: Rising Above Illusion

As Krishna's discourse unfolds, Arjuna gradually **overcomes his despair** and understands the **eternal nature of the soul (Atman), the impermanence of the body, and the necessity of performing one's duty selflessly.** The Bhagavad Gita teaches that:

- **Life is a battlefield where everyone must face challenges with courage and wisdom.**

- **Action (Karma) must be performed without attachment to results (Karma Yoga).**

- **True knowledge (Jnana) leads to liberation from fear and doubt.**

- **Devotion to the Divine (Bhakti Yoga) grants inner peace and fulfillment.**

In the end, Arjuna **picks up his bow again**, ready to fight—not out of hatred, but with a **clear understanding**

of his purpose. The battle begins, but with Arjuna transformed from a confused warrior into an enlightened soul, ready to act with **duty, faith, and wisdom.**

Conclusion: The Battlefield as a Metaphor for Life

The **Kurukshetra battlefield**, as depicted in the **Bhagavad Gita**, is not just an external war but an **internal spiritual battle** that every human being must fight. Arjuna's dilemma represents the universal struggles of doubt, fear, and moral conflict. Krishna's teachings provide **timeless wisdom**, guiding humanity toward a life of **righteousness, courage, and self-realization.**

The Bhagavad Gita remains relevant even today, as **each person faces their own Kurukshetra, struggling with choices, responsibilities, and ethical dilemmas.** The ultimate message of the Gita is that **one must rise above illusion, act with wisdom, and surrender to the divine, thereby achieving true liberation (Moksha).**

Chapter 02: The Concept of Dharma: The Path of Righteousness

1 Understanding Dharma in Different Contexts

Dharma, a fundamental concept in Hindu philosophy, is an all-encompassing principle that governs moral law, righteousness, duty, and cosmic order. The word 'Dharma' is derived from the Sanskrit root 'Dhri,' meaning 'to uphold' or 'to sustain.' In Hinduism, Dharma is dynamic, varying according to context, individual responsibilities, and stages of life. It is essential for maintaining harmony in the universe and ensuring spiritual progress. The concept of Dharma is deeply embedded in Hindu texts, including the Vedas, Upanishads, Bhagavad Gita, and the epics Ramayana and Mahabharata. This document explores the various Hindu contexts in which Dharma operates, including individual Dharma (Svadharma), social Dharma (Varna and Ashrama Dharma), universal Dharma (Sanatana Dharma), and situational Dharma (Apad Dharma).

Dharma in the Vedic Tradition

Dharma, a core concept in Hindu philosophy, finds its earliest expressions in the **Vedic tradition**, where it is deeply interwoven with cosmic order, ritual duties, and moral obligations. The **Vedas**, the oldest scriptures of Hinduism, lay the foundation for understanding Dharma as the principle that maintains harmony in the universe. Derived from the Sanskrit root **"dhṛ"**, meaning **"to uphold" or "to sustain,"** Dharma in the Vedic era was closely linked to **Rta**, the cosmic law that governs all existence. This concept later evolved into a more structured system of ethical and social duties.

Rta: The Cosmic Order

In the **Rigveda**, one of the oldest Vedic texts, Dharma is often equated with **Rta**, the divine order that regulates the universe. Rta is responsible for maintaining the cycles of nature, the movement of celestial bodies, and the balance between truth and justice. The gods, particularly **Varuna**, the guardian of cosmic law, are seen as upholders of Rta, ensuring that it remains unbroken. Human beings, through their actions, are expected to align with this cosmic order, thus adhering to Dharma.

The Role of Yajna (Sacrifice) in Dharma

One of the most significant aspects of Dharma in the Vedic tradition is the **performance of Yajna (sacrificial rituals).** These rituals were believed to sustain cosmic balance and appease the gods. The **Yajurveda** and **Samaveda** provide elaborate instructions on conducting these sacrifices, highlighting the idea that Dharma is not just an individual pursuit but a collective responsibility. The **priests (Brahmins)** played a crucial role in ensuring that the right mantras, offerings, and procedures were followed, reinforcing the idea that adherence to ritualistic duties was essential for maintaining Dharma.

Dharma and Social Order (Varna System)

The Vedic texts also laid the groundwork for the **Varna system**, which classified society into four groups— **Brahmins (priests and scholars), Kshatriyas (warriors**

and rulers), Vaishyas (merchants and agriculturists), and Shudras (laborers and service providers). Each Varna had its specific **Svadharma (personal duty)** that contributed to the overall functioning of society. This division was not originally meant to be rigid but was based on one's qualities and actions (**Guna and Karma**). Over time, however, this system became hereditary and more rigidly structured.

Dharma and Moral Conduct in the Vedic Age

Apart from rituals and social duties, Dharma in the Vedic tradition also encompassed **ethical behavior, truthfulness (Satya), non-violence (Ahimsa), and hospitality (Atithi Devo Bhava).** The **Rigveda** and **Atharvaveda** emphasize the importance of truth and righteousness, suggesting that adherence to Dharma leads to prosperity and divine blessings. The **Upanishads**, which are later Vedic texts, begin to shift the focus from external rituals to inner self-discipline, wisdom, and self-realization, thus evolving the concept of Dharma beyond mere ritualism.

Conclusion

Dharma in the Vedic tradition is an all-encompassing principle that governs **cosmic law, social order, religious duties, and moral behavior.** It is rooted in the idea that individuals must act in accordance with **Rta** to maintain harmony in the world. The later Hindu scriptures, including the **Mahabharata, Ramayana, and Bhagavad Gita**, build upon these foundational ideas, refining the concept of Dharma into a more philosophical and practical doctrine. This evolution marks the transition of Dharma from being solely ritualistic to a guiding force in human life, shaping Hindu ethics and spirituality for centuries.

Dharma in the Bhagavad Gita: Svadharma vs. Sanatana Dharma

The Bhagavad Gita presents a profound discourse on Dharma, distinguishing between **Svadharma** (one's personal duty) and **Sanatana Dharma** (the eternal universal order). These concepts play a central role in Krishna's guidance to Arjuna, shaping the philosophical and ethical foundation of the Gita.

Svadharma: The Individual's Duty

Svadharma refers to the duty assigned to an individual based on their inherent nature, skills, and societal role. In the Gita, Krishna emphasizes that one must follow their own Dharma, even if it appears flawed, rather than undertaking another's duty, which might seem superior but is not aligned with one's true nature. This idea is deeply connected to the **Varna system**, where individuals perform roles based on their disposition and upbringing. Krishna tells Arjuna (BG 3.35):

"Better is one's own duty, though imperfect, than the duty of another well performed. Death in one's own Dharma is better; the duty of another is fraught with fear."

Arjuna's **Svadharma** as a Kshatriya is to fight in the righteous battle, but his hesitation stems from emotional attachments and personal dilemmas. Krishna urges him to rise above these attachments and fulfill his duty selflessly, without concern for personal gain or loss.

Sanatana Dharma: The Eternal Universal Order

While Svadharma focuses on individual responsibility, **Sanatana Dharma** refers to the eternal principles that govern the universe. It encompasses righteousness, truth, compassion, and selfless service, applicable to all beings regardless of their social role. Krishna reveals that the ultimate Dharma is **devotion to the divine, selfless service, and spiritual wisdom**. He states (BG 18.66):

"Abandon all varieties of Dharma and simply surrender unto Me. I shall deliver you from all sinful reactions. Do not fear."

This verse suggests that beyond social duties, there exists a higher Dharma rooted in **divine surrender and self-realization**. Krishna teaches that **real Dharma transcends material designations** and leads the soul toward liberation (**Moksha**).

Reconciling Svadharma and Sanatana Dharma

The Gita does not propose a conflict between these two forms of Dharma but rather a **synthesis**. Following Svadharma with **detachment from results (Nishkama Karma Yoga)** aligns an individual with the higher order of Sanatana Dharma. By performing duties with **selflessness and devotion**, one progresses spiritually while contributing to societal harmony.

Modern Implications of Svadharma and Sanatana Dharma

In today's world, the distinction between Svadharma and Sanatana Dharma remains relevant. Individuals must balance **professional duties, personal responsibilities, and ethical principles** while striving for inner harmony. Whether in career choices, social responsibilities, or spiritual pursuits, Krishna's teachings encourage action with **righteousness, integrity, and devotion**.

The Bhagavad Gita thus provides a universal framework for understanding Dharma, showing that **true righteousness lies not in rigid adherence to duties but in selfless action guided by wisdom and devotion**.

Varna Dharma: The Role of Caste in Determining Duty

Dharma in Hinduism is often intertwined with the concept of **Varna Dharma**, which defines duty based on one's caste or social classification. This system, as articulated in Hindu scriptures like the **Manusmriti** and **Bhagavad Gita**, divides society into four primary varnas: **Brahmins (priests and scholars), Kshatriyas (warriors and rulers), Vaishyas (merchants and agriculturalists), and Shudras (laborers and service providers).** Each of these groups is assigned specific duties aligned with their natural tendencies and societal roles, ensuring the smooth functioning of society.

The Bhagavad Gita (Chapter 18, Verses 41-44) affirms that each individual has an inherent duty, determined by their qualities (guna) and actions (karma), rather than mere birth. Krishna explains that **Brahmins** are predisposed to knowledge and spirituality, **Kshatriyas** to courage and governance, **Vaishyas** to commerce and agriculture, and **Shudras** to service. The principle of **Svadharma** (one's personal duty) within the Varna system suggests that fulfillment and righteousness come from adhering to the role suited to one's inner disposition.

However, Varna Dharma has been a topic of **philosophical and ethical debate**. While ancient texts presented it as a **fluid system based on qualities and actions**, it later became a rigid hereditary structure, leading to social discrimination. Reformers like **Swami Vivekananda, Mahatma Gandhi, and Dr. B.R. Ambedkar** critiqued this rigidity, advocating for a more egalitarian interpretation of Dharma. Many modern interpretations of Hinduism emphasize that **Dharma should be based on merit, ethical conduct, and service to humanity rather than caste.**

In the **contemporary world**, the relevance of Varna Dharma has shifted. While traditional duties are no longer strictly followed, the principle that **one's duty should align with their skills, strengths, and contributions to society** remains significant. For instance, a teacher, doctor, or soldier may embody the spirit of **Brahmin, Kshatriya, or Vaishya dharma**, regardless of birth. The Bhagavad Gita's guidance that one should perform their **Svadharma with dedication, without attachment to results,** continues to inspire individuals to act ethically and responsibly in their professions and personal lives.

Despite historical challenges, the essence of Varna Dharma can still offer a **pragmatic approach to social responsibility** when interpreted through a lens of justice and equality. The evolving understanding of **Dharma in modern Hinduism** leans toward inclusivity, focusing on individual duty based on skills and ethical values rather than rigid caste divisions. Thus, the concept of Varna Dharma, while rooted in ancient texts, continues to be reinterpreted to align with contemporary human values and social justice ideals.

Dharma is linked to the Varna system, which classifies individuals into four groups:

- **Brahmins (Priests and Scholars)** – Their Dharma is to study, teach, and uphold spiritual wisdom.

- **Kshatriyas (Warriors and Rulers)** – Their Dharma is to protect society and uphold justice.

- **Vaishyas (Merchants and Farmers)** – Their Dharma is to engage in commerce and agricultural activities.

- **Shudras (Laborers and Servants)** – Their Dharma is to provide service to society. Though the Varna system was originally based on qualities and occupation rather than birth, it later became rigid, leading to social stratification. The Bhagavad Gita reinterprets Varna Dharma as being based on individual nature (Guna) and actions (Karma), emphasizing the fluidity of one's duties.

Ashrama Dharma: Duties According to Stages of Life

Hindu tradition divides human life into four stages (**Ashramas**), each with specific duties:

- **Brahmacharya (Student Life)** – This stage focuses on learning, discipline, and self-control. A

Brahmachari (student) is expected to live a celibate life, study the scriptures under a guru, and develop physical, mental, and moral strength. The foundation of a righteous life is laid in this stage through education and character-building.

- **Grihastha (Householder Life)** – This is the stage of fulfilling familial, professional, and social responsibilities. A Grihastha (householder) is expected to earn a living ethically, support family members, perform religious duties, and contribute to society. This stage upholds Dharma by balancing material pursuits with moral obligations.

- **Vanaprastha (Retirement/Forest Dweller Stage)** – In this stage, individuals gradually withdraw from worldly duties and turn toward spiritual pursuits. Traditionally, this meant retreating to the forest to meditate and study scriptures, but in modern times, it symbolizes reducing material attachments and engaging in acts of charity, self-reflection, and guidance for the younger generation.

- **Sannyasa (Renunciation)** – The final stage involves complete renunciation of material attachments and a sole focus on attaining Moksha (liberation). A Sannyasi (renunciant) relinquishes personal possessions, relationships, and desires, dedicating life entirely to spiritual enlightenment and service to humanity.

Each stage carries unique **Dharmic responsibilities**, ensuring a balanced and spiritually fulfilling life. This structured progression provides a **holistic approach to life**, integrating ethical living, material responsibilities, and spiritual evolution.

Raja Dharma: The Duty of Kings and Governance

Raja Dharma (the duty of kings) forms a crucial aspect of Hindu political philosophy, outlining the responsibilities of rulers in maintaining **justice, righteousness, and prosperity** in society. Ancient Hindu scriptures such as the **Mahabharata, Manusmriti, and Arthashastra** provide detailed guidelines on how a king should govern with wisdom, fairness, and devotion to Dharma.

- **The King as the Protector of Dharma** The primary duty of a king is to uphold **Dharma (righteousness)** and ensure that society functions in harmony. He must protect his people from internal and external threats, enforce justice, and uphold the moral order. The Mahabharata states that a **just ruler ensures the welfare of his subjects, placing their needs above his own personal desires**.

- **Justice and Law Enforcement** A king is responsible for enforcing **Danda (law and punishment)** to maintain order. The Manusmriti emphasizes that a just ruler must punish wrongdoers while being compassionate and fair. The **Arthashastra**, written by **Chanakya (Kautilya),** provides a pragmatic approach to governance, advocating for a balance between strict law enforcement and welfare policies.

- **Duties in Warfare and Diplomacy** A Kshatriya king must defend his kingdom and uphold peace through diplomacy. The **Bhagavad Gita's message to Arjuna** highlights that a warrior's duty is to fight **righteously** without attachment to personal gain. The Arthashastra further explains strategies of war, alliances, and governance, emphasizing that **true leadership is about ensuring stability and prosperity.**

- **Welfare of the People** Good governance requires the king to act as a **caretaker** of his people, providing for their education, healthcare, and economic well-being. The **Mahabharata** describes a **Dharmic ruler** as one who serves his people selflessly, promotes justice, and ensures no one suffers from hunger or oppression.

- **Moral and Spiritual Leadership** A ruler must be a role model of **righteousness, wisdom, and self-discipline**. Kings were often expected to seek the guidance of **sages and spiritual leaders** to rule in accordance with Dharma. The ideal ruler is one who governs with **compassion, fairness, and adherence to divine wisdom.**

In contemporary times, the principles of **Raja Dharma** can be applied to leadership roles in government, business, and social administration, emphasizing **ethical governance, justice, and public welfare.**

Apad Dharma: Dharma in Times of Crisis

In Hindu philosophy, **Apad Dharma** refers to the ethical and moral guidelines that apply in times of crisis or emergency. The term "Apad" means calamity or distress, and "Dharma" signifies duty or righteousness. While Dharma is generally associated with upholding moral order, Apad Dharma acknowledges that extraordinary situations require flexibility in ethical conduct. It serves as a guiding principle for navigating unforeseen circumstances while maintaining a deeper commitment to righteousness.

The Need for Apad Dharma

Life is unpredictable, and individuals, communities, and rulers often face crises that challenge their ability to adhere to traditional Dharma. Natural disasters, war, economic collapse, personal adversity, or social upheaval may create circumstances where strict adherence to conventional duties becomes impractical or even harmful. Hindu scriptures recognize that, in such situations, adjustments must be made without entirely abandoning moral principles. **Apad Dharma provides a framework to ensure survival and social stability while maintaining ethical integrity.**

Scriptural References and Examples

The concept of Apad Dharma is deeply embedded in Hindu scriptures, including the Mahabharata, Manusmriti, and the Bhagavad Gita. These texts offer guidance on adapting moral responsibilities in times of hardship.

- **Mahabharata and Apad Dharma:** One of the most profound discussions of Apad Dharma occurs in the Mahabharata. When Yudhishthira, the eldest Pandava, asks Bhishma about the duties of a king in times of crisis, Bhishma explains that **preserving life and stability takes precedence over conventional duties.** He advises that a king may adopt unorthodox methods, including deception, if necessary, to protect his people and kingdom. The Pandavas themselves embody Apad Dharma during their exile. Disguising themselves in King Virata's court, they temporarily set aside their royal duties to ensure survival.

- **Manusmriti and Emergency Ethics:** The Manusmriti, a key text on Hindu law, discusses how duties and social roles may be altered in exceptional times. It allows for Brahmins, who traditionally should not engage in trade or warfare, to take up such occupations during crises if it ensures their survival. However, they are expected to return to their prescribed duties once normalcy is restored.

- **Krishna's Counsel to Arjuna:** In the Bhagavad Gita, Krishna advises Arjuna that Dharma is dynamic and must be understood in context. In the battlefield scenario, Arjuna's Dharma as a warrior (Kshatriya Dharma) takes precedence over his personal reluctance to fight. This is an example of Apad Dharma, where duty is reinterpreted in light of extraordinary circumstances.

Flexibility and Moral Decision-Making

Apad Dharma does not advocate unethical behavior but recognizes that **moral rigidity can sometimes lead to greater harm.** It allows individuals to make pragmatic decisions while ensuring that their actions align with a larger ethical vision. **For example:**

- A doctor in wartime may need to prioritize saving the most critical patients rather than strictly following hospital protocols.

- A king or political leader may need to deceive an enemy to protect the state, even though deception is generally discouraged.

- A person facing financial ruin due to an economic crisis may take up an unconventional job, even if it contradicts their Varna Dharma.

Modern-Day Applications of Apad Dharma

The principles of Apad Dharma remain highly relevant today. In modern life, crises such as **pandemics, wars, economic recessions, and personal emergencies** often demand flexibility in ethical decision-making.

- **Healthcare and Ethics:** During medical crises like the COVID-19 pandemic, doctors and policymakers had to prioritize limited resources, making difficult choices about who would receive medical attention first. These decisions align with the principles of Apad Dharma—adapting moral action to circumstances.

- **Legal and Political Scenarios:** In governance, leaders often face dilemmas where they must **balance individual rights with national security**. For instance, during national emergencies, governments may impose temporary restrictions on freedoms for the greater good.
- **Personal Ethics in Crisis:** In personal life, individuals may need to compromise on their usual moral standards to survive. A vegetarian stranded in a place with no food options may eat non-vegetarian food to sustain themselves, understanding that survival is a higher duty in that moment.

Conclusion

Apad Dharma underscores the adaptability of moral and ethical principles in Hindu philosophy. It teaches that righteousness is not about rigidly adhering to laws but about **acting in a way that preserves life, justice, and long-term Dharma**. This concept ensures that individuals and societies can navigate crises without losing sight of their core ethical values. By understanding and applying Apad Dharma, one can uphold the spirit of righteousness even in the most challenging situations.

Dharma and Karma: The Interplay of Duty and Consequence

Dharma and Karma are two fundamental concepts in Hindu philosophy, intricately linked in shaping human life. **Dharma** refers to one's righteous duty and moral order, while **Karma** signifies action and its consequences. The interplay between the two establishes a framework where fulfilling one's duty leads to positive outcomes, whereas neglecting or violating Dharma results in adverse consequences. This connection reinforces the ethical dimension of Hindu thought, emphasizing responsibility, moral conduct, and spiritual evolution.

The Relationship Between Dharma and Karma

In Hindu tradition, **Karma is the fruit of Dharma**. The Bhagavad Gita emphasizes the idea of **Nishkama Karma**—selfless action performed in accordance with Dharma, without attachment to the results. Lord Krishna advises Arjuna to act in accordance with his Dharma as a warrior (Kshatriya), reinforcing that one's duty must be performed regardless of personal desires or fears. This principle ensures the sustenance of cosmic balance (Rta) and aligns individuals with the divine order.

Karma operates under the principle of **cause and effect**—every action has repercussions that determine one's present and future circumstances. Good actions aligned with Dharma yield positive Karma, leading to spiritual growth and eventual liberation (Moksha). Conversely, actions driven by selfishness, greed, or neglect of Dharma generate negative Karma, resulting in suffering and reincarnation cycles (Samsara).

Types of Karma and Their Dharmic Implications

Hindu philosophy classifies Karma into three main types, each influencing Dharma:

- **Sanchita Karma** – The accumulated Karma from past lives, influencing one's present circumstances. Dharma guides individuals on how to mitigate its effects through righteous living.
- **Prarabdha Karma** – The portion of past Karma that is currently unfolding in one's life. Adhering to Dharma helps navigate its challenges.
- **Kriyamana Karma** – The Karma created by present actions, shaping future experiences. Following Dharma ensures that present choices lead to positive future outcomes.

Balancing Dharma and Karma in Daily Life

The interplay between Dharma and Karma extends beyond scriptures into everyday decision-making. Ethical dilemmas often require balancing personal desires with societal duties. For example, a doctor's Dharma is to save lives, even if it means personal risk. Similarly, a businessperson must uphold honesty and fairness despite challenges.

In modern society, understanding this relationship fosters a sense of accountability, encouraging individuals to act selflessly, uphold integrity, and contribute positively to the world. By aligning one's actions with Dharma, one not only cultivates good Karma but also paves the path toward spiritual fulfillment and liberation.

Ultimately, Dharma and Karma function as **two sides of the same coin**, guiding individuals toward a life of righteousness, responsibility, and ultimate transcendence. Their harmonious integration ensures not only personal well-being but also the greater good of society and the cosmic order.

Dharma in Bhakti and Jnana Traditions

The concept of **Dharma** is one of the most fundamental aspects of Hindu philosophy, shaping ethical, social, and spiritual duties. Within Hinduism, the paths of **Bhakti (devotion)** and **Jnana (knowledge)** offer two distinct yet complementary approaches to understanding and practicing Dharma. While Bhakti emphasizes **loving devotion to a personal deity**, Jnana focuses on **self-inquiry and realization of the ultimate truth (Brahman).** Despite their differences, both traditions guide adherents toward a righteous life, with Dharma serving as a crucial bridge between spiritual practice and worldly responsibilities.

Bhakti Tradition: Dharma as Loving Devotion

Bhakti Yoga, or the path of devotion, centers on **surrendering oneself to a chosen deity**, believing that unwavering faith and love lead to ultimate liberation (Moksha). Dharma, in this tradition, is often expressed through **selfless service, prayer, and ethical conduct** in devotion to God. The Bhagavad Gita, particularly in chapters 9 and 12, highlights Bhakti as one of the highest paths, emphasizing **faith, humility, and unconditional love** as core Dharmic duties.

- **Dharma as Loving Service** – In Bhakti, the highest duty is serving God with a pure heart. Devotees engage in **worship (puja), singing hymns (kirtan), and remembering the divine**

(smarana) as expressions of their Dharmic responsibility. This aligns with the idea that righteous living involves continuous remembrance and devotion.

- **The Role of Divine Grace** – Unlike karma-based traditions where **actions lead to consequences**, Bhakti traditions often emphasize **grace (Kripa)**. The devotee's primary Dharma is **surrendering (Sharanagati)** to the divine will, believing that God's mercy transcends karmic bondage.

- **Ethical and Social Dharma in Bhakti** – Devotional texts like the Bhagavata Purana encourage **compassion, non-violence, honesty, and humility**, demonstrating that devotion should be accompanied by righteous actions. Saints like **Mirabai, Tulsidas, and Chaitanya Mahaprabhu** exemplified Bhakti Dharma by practicing devotion while upholding moral values.

- **Dharma Beyond Rituals** – Bhakti emphasizes an **internalized Dharma**, where the devotee transcends rigid ritualistic obligations in favor of **sincere devotion**. The Bhagavad Gita (9.26) states that even **a simple offering made with love** is accepted by God, reinforcing that Bhakti Dharma prioritizes inner sincerity over external formalities.

Jnana Tradition: Dharma as Knowledge and Realization

Jnana Yoga, the path of wisdom, defines Dharma as **the pursuit of truth (Satya) and the realization of the self**

(Atman) as Brahman. This tradition, rooted in **Advaita Vedanta and Upanishadic teachings**, considers Dharma as a means to transcend illusion (Maya) and attain self-realization.

- **Dharma as Self-Inquiry** – The ultimate duty in Jnana tradition is **discerning the real from the unreal (Viveka)**. Scriptures like the Upanishads and the teachings of Adi Shankaracharya advocate self-reflection, meditation, and detachment as essential Dharmic duties.
- **Renunciation and Inner Dharma** – Unlike Bhakti, which emphasizes **active devotion**, Jnana Yoga often leads to **renunciation (Sannyasa)**. Here, Dharma is less about social responsibilities and more about **internal discipline, contemplation, and realization of the eternal self**.
- **Ethics and Dharma in Jnana Yoga** – Even though Jnana emphasizes self-knowledge, it does not reject ethical living. The pursuit of knowledge must be accompanied by **truthfulness (Satya), non-violence (Ahimsa), patience (Kshama), and self-control (Dama)**—virtues considered integral to a wise person's Dharma.
- **Liberation as the Ultimate Dharma** – In Jnana tradition, the highest duty is realizing that **the self (Atman) is identical to Brahman**. This realization dissolves ego and attachments, leading to freedom from karma and rebirth (Moksha). Thus, the **greatest Dharma in Jnana Yoga is to**

transcend worldly dualities and achieve spiritual enlightenment.

Interplay Between Bhakti and Jnana Dharma

Though Bhakti and Jnana take different approaches, they ultimately converge. The Bhagavad Gita (7.16-19) describes how **devotion (Bhakti) matures into wisdom (Jnana)**, suggesting that a true devotee also attains self-knowledge. Similarly, **Adi Shankaracharya**, a proponent of Jnana, acknowledged that Bhakti can be a stepping stone to wisdom.

- **Devotion Leading to Wisdom** – Many saints, including **Ramanuja and Vallabhacharya**, argued that **Jnana without Bhakti is dry intellectualism**, while Bhakti infused with wisdom leads to **higher spiritual realization**.
- **The Role of Karma Yoga** – The Bhagavad Gita integrates both Bhakti and Jnana with **Karma Yoga (selfless action)**, emphasizing that **one's Dharma is to act selflessly, guided by devotion and wisdom**.

Dharma in Bhakti and Jnana traditions reflects **two complementary spiritual paths**—one of **love and surrender**, the other of **knowledge and discernment**. While Bhakti emphasizes **serving and loving God as the highest duty**, Jnana upholds **self-realization and wisdom as the supreme Dharma**. Both traditions, however, recognize ethical living, self-discipline, and spiritual dedication as essential components of a Dharmic life. In the end, whether through devotion or knowledge,

Dharma leads one toward **truth, righteousness, and ultimate liberation (Moksha).**

Modern Reinterpretations of Dharma

Dharma, traditionally understood as duty, righteousness, and moral order, has undergone significant reinterpretation in the modern era. While rooted in ancient Hindu scriptures, the concept of Dharma has evolved to address contemporary challenges, ethical dilemmas, and shifting societal values. Today, Dharma is no longer confined to rigid caste-based duties or scriptural injunctions but is understood as a fluid and adaptable moral compass guiding individuals and societies toward justice, harmony, and self-realization.

Dharma in Secular and Global Contexts

In the modern secular world, Dharma extends beyond religious obligations and integrates into universal ethics. Philosophers, social reformers, and leaders interpret Dharma as a sense of responsibility that transcends personal gains and aligns with the welfare of humanity. In this sense, Dharma aligns closely with universal human rights, social justice, and environmental sustainability.

For instance, Mahatma Gandhi redefined Dharma as the pursuit of truth (**Satya**) and nonviolence (**Ahimsa**). He emphasized that Dharma is not limited to religious duties but extends to ethical living and the fight for justice. His doctrine of **Satyagraha** (truth-force) was a Dharmic response to colonial oppression, illustrating how Dharma can be applied to socio-political struggles.

Dharma and Individual Autonomy

Traditionally, Dharma was prescribed according to Varna (caste) and Ashrama (stage of life), often limiting personal choice. However, in contemporary society, Dharma is increasingly associated with **individual ethics, personal responsibility, and inner calling** (Svadharma). Unlike rigid adherence to caste-based roles, modern interpretations emphasize that Dharma should be discovered by each individual based on their conscience, education, and life circumstances.

For example, professionals in various fields interpret Dharma as ethical responsibility:

- A doctor's Dharma is to heal without discrimination.

- A journalist's Dharma is to report truthfully.

- A business leader's Dharma is to uphold integrity and corporate responsibility.

This individualized approach aligns with **existential and humanistic philosophies**, which emphasize personal choice and self-determined purpose.

Dharma and Gender Equality

Classical Hindu traditions often prescribed different Dharmic duties for men and women, reinforcing patriarchal norms. However, modern reinterpretations advocate for **gender equality** and question discriminatory traditions.

Contemporary Hindu scholars and feminists argue that Dharma must evolve to promote social justice. Figures like Swami Vivekananda emphasized that women should pursue education and self-reliance as part of their Dharma. Today, the Dharma of women is no longer confined to household duties but includes leadership, education, and self-empowerment.

Dharma and Environmental Ethics

In the face of climate change and ecological crises, Dharma has been reinterpreted to include **environmental responsibility**. Hindu texts have long emphasized the sanctity of nature—concepts such as **Vasudhaiva Kutumbakam** (the world is one family) and **Ahimsa** (non-violence) extend to the treatment of the environment.

Modern environmental movements draw upon these Dharmic principles, advocating for sustainable living, conservation, and ethical treatment of animals. Organizations like the **Chipko Movement** (tree-hugging movement in India) embody this ecological Dharma, reinforcing the idea that protecting nature is a moral duty.

Dharma in the Digital Age

The rise of technology and digital culture has introduced new ethical dilemmas. Questions of **privacy, misinformation, cyber ethics, and digital addiction** challenge traditional notions of Dharma. The responsibility of using technology ethically is now considered a form of modern Dharma.

For example:

- Social media influencers bear the Dharma of **truthful representation**.

- Developers and AI researchers have a Dharmic responsibility to ensure ethical programming.

- Citizens engaging in digital activism must balance free speech with **social responsibility**.

Modern reinterpretations of Dharma reflect the evolving nature of human societies. While the essence of Dharma as righteousness and duty remains, its application has expanded to include **social justice, environmental responsibility, gender equality, and ethical technology use**. This dynamic understanding ensures that Dharma remains relevant, offering a moral foundation for addressing contemporary challenges. As society continues to evolve, so too will Dharma, serving as an adaptable guide for ethical living in an ever-changing world.

Conclusion

Dharma remains a dynamic and evolving concept in Hindu thought, adapting to changing times while preserving its core essence of righteousness and duty. Whether in personal conduct, governance, or spiritual practice, Dharma provides a guiding framework for ethical living. Understanding Dharma in its diverse Hindu contexts allows for a more profound appreciation of its role in shaping individual and collective destiny.

2 Duty vs. Desire: Krishna's Guidance to Arjuna

The Bhagavad Gita, a sacred Hindu scripture, is a profound dialogue between Lord Krishna and Arjuna on the battlefield of Kurukshetra. This conversation encapsulates the eternal conflict between duty (dharma) and desire (kama). As Arjuna, a mighty warrior, hesitates to fight against his own relatives, teachers, and loved ones, Krishna offers him divine wisdom, illuminating the path of righteousness. This discourse serves as a timeless guide for individuals torn between personal emotions and moral obligations.

Arjuna's Dilemma: The Conflict of Duty and Emotion

As the great war of Mahabharata was about to begin, Arjuna, standing in his chariot, observed both armies. The sight of his own relatives, revered teachers, and dear friends lined up on both sides filled his heart with an overwhelming sense of grief and despair. His hands trembled, his bow slipped from his grasp, and his mind was clouded with confusion. How could he lift his weapon against those he had respected and loved all his life? How could a war that would bring such immense destruction ever be justified?

Arjuna's internal turmoil reflected the broader human struggle of choosing between duty and personal emotions. He was not merely concerned with winning or losing; he was tormented by the morality of his actions. The thought of killing his own family members and mentors felt unbearable. He feared that by engaging in battle, he would be committing an unforgivable sin, leading to the destruction of his lineage and the moral decay of society.

Furthermore, Arjuna worried about the repercussions of war on future generations. He foresaw the devastation that would follow, including the loss of countless lives and the breakdown of societal values. He feared that the absence of righteous men would lead to chaos, lawlessness, and the corruption of traditions. His anguish was not just personal but deeply rooted in his sense of responsibility toward his people.

In his despair, Arjuna questioned the very purpose of life and duty. He wondered whether victory, kingdom, and power held any meaning when achieved at the cost of immense suffering. His heart longed for an alternative path—one that did not require him to choose between love and responsibility, between compassion and duty. It was at this moment of vulnerability that Arjuna turned to Krishna for guidance, seeking wisdom beyond his mortal understanding.

Krishna, witnessing Arjuna's paralysis, responded with a profound discourse that transcended the battlefield. He reminded Arjuna that his hesitation stemmed from attachment and ignorance. Krishna urged him to look beyond temporary emotions and recognize his higher duty as a warrior—to uphold righteousness and justice. He explained that true wisdom lies in understanding the eternal nature of the soul and acting in alignment with one's dharma without fear or hesitation.

This pivotal moment in the Bhagavad Gita is not just a lesson for Arjuna but for all of humanity. It teaches us that in times of crisis, we must rise above personal desires and emotions to fulfill our higher purpose. Arjuna's dilemma mirrors the struggles faced by individuals in various walks of life, where difficult decisions must be made by prioritizing duty over fleeting emotions.

Krishna's Teachings: The Path of Selfless Action

Krishna's response to Arjuna's dilemma is centered on selfless action, known as **Nishkama Karma**. He urges Arjuna to perform his duty without attachment to rewards. This philosophy is deeply rooted in several fundamental teachings:

1. **Nishkama Karma (Selfless Action):** Krishna emphasizes that one should act according to their duty without desire for the fruits of their labor. True fulfillment lies in selfless service, and attachment to outcomes leads to suffering. By surrendering personal ambitions and focusing on righteousness, one attains inner peace and liberation (moksha).

2. **Swadharma (One's Own Duty):** Krishna teaches that every individual has a unique duty based on their nature and role in society. Arjuna, as a Kshatriya (warrior), is bound to fight for justice. Avoiding one's duty due to fear or attachment is detrimental to personal and societal well-being.

3. **Atman (The Eternal Soul):** Krishna reassures Arjuna that the soul is immortal and indestructible. While the physical body perishes,

the soul continues its journey. Thus, grieving for the dead is unnecessary, and performing duty with this understanding brings spiritual clarity.

4. **Sthitaprajna (Equanimity):** Krishna encourages Arjuna to maintain a balanced mind in success and failure, pleasure and pain. A true seeker of wisdom remains undisturbed by external circumstances, focusing solely on righteous action.

5. **Yoga (Union with the Divine):** Krishna introduces various paths of yoga to achieve spiritual enlightenment:

   o **Karma Yoga (Path of Action):** Performing duties selflessly without attachment.

   o **Bhakti Yoga (Path of Devotion):** Surrendering oneself to divine will through devotion and faith.

   o **Jnana Yoga (Path of Knowledge):** Seeking ultimate truth through wisdom and self-inquiry.

6. **Overcoming Desires:** Krishna warns that uncontrolled desires lead to greed, anger, and ignorance, which cloud judgment. By mastering one's desires and acting with self-discipline, one attains true wisdom and liberation from worldly suffering.

7. **Detachment and Devotion:** Krishna explains that by surrendering ego and acting in devotion to the divine, one transcends worldly struggles. True freedom lies in detachment from material gains and unwavering faith in the higher purpose of life.

Overcoming Desire: The Road to Liberation

Desire, according to Krishna, is the root cause of suffering. When one is consumed by personal wants and attachments, they become trapped in an endless cycle of birth and rebirth (samsara). By surrendering desires and embracing duty with detachment, one achieves inner peace.

The Nature of Desire

Desires arise from sensory experiences, emotions, and attachments. They are driven by the mind's inclination toward pleasure and aversion to pain. While certain desires, such as the need for food and shelter, are essential for survival, unchecked longing for material gains and pleasures creates bondage.

Krishna explains to Arjuna that desires function like fire—when fueled, they grow uncontrollable. The constant pursuit of gratification leads to frustration and dissatisfaction because no worldly pleasure is permanent. This endless cycle binds individuals to suffering, preventing them from attaining higher wisdom and peace.

The Consequences of Uncontrolled Desire

1. **Attachment and Fear:** The more one desires, the more they become attached to outcomes. This

attachment breeds fear—fear of loss, failure, and uncertainty.

2. **Mental Agitation**: Desires, when unmet, lead to frustration, anger, and restlessness, disturbing inner harmony.

3. **Karma and Rebirth**: Actions driven by selfish desires create karma, prolonging the cycle of birth and rebirth.

4. **Moral Degradation**: Excessive desire often pushes individuals toward unethical actions, fostering greed, dishonesty, and exploitation.

Krishna's Teachings on Overcoming Desire

Krishna urges Arjuna to rise above temporary emotions and embrace his divine responsibility. He reassures Arjuna that true liberation comes from performing one's duty without hesitation or selfish intent. The Bhagavad Gita outlines various methods to master desires and attain inner peace:

1. Nishkama Karma (Selfless Action)

Krishna emphasizes that performing one's duty without attachment to rewards leads to spiritual liberation. Desire binds individuals to the fruits of their actions, whereas selfless action fosters detachment and purity of mind.

Practical Steps:

- Focus on doing your best rather than obsessing over results.

- Serve others without expecting recognition or rewards.

- Approach work as a means of self-improvement rather than personal gain.

2. Cultivating Self-Control and Discipline

Krishna advises mastering the senses rather than being controlled by them. A disciplined mind resists impulsive desires and remains steadfast in righteousness.

Practical Steps:

- Practice meditation to gain control over impulses.

- Avoid excessive indulgence in material pleasures.

- Develop a balanced lifestyle with moderation in food, speech, and actions.

3. Understanding the Eternal Soul (Atman)

Krishna teaches that the soul (Atman) is eternal, beyond physical desires. Identifying with the body leads to craving, whereas realizing one's spiritual nature frees the mind from material attachments.

Practical Steps:

- Contemplate the transient nature of worldly pleasures.

- Read spiritual texts to develop a deeper understanding of the self.

- Seek inner fulfillment rather than external validation.

4. Developing Equanimity (Sthitaprajna)

Krishna advises maintaining equanimity in success and failure, pleasure and pain. A wise person remains undisturbed by external circumstances, finding joy in self-awareness rather than material achievements.

Practical Steps:

- Accept life's ups and downs with a balanced mind.

- Avoid extreme emotional reactions to situations.

- Cultivate gratitude and mindfulness in daily life.

5. Bhakti Yoga (Path of Devotion)

Krishna highlights devotion (bhakti) as a means of overcoming desires. Surrendering to the divine allows individuals to transcend material cravings and experience divine love and contentment.

Practical Steps:

- Engage in prayer, chanting, or meditation focused on the divine.

- Cultivate faith and surrender to a higher purpose.

- Practice loving service to others as an expression of devotion.

The Ultimate Liberation: Attaining Moksha

Krishna explains that by mastering desires, one attains **moksha**, liberation from the cycle of birth and death. When the mind is free from selfish cravings, it experiences true bliss. The key lies in transcending temporary emotions and aligning oneself with eternal wisdom.

By following Krishna's teachings, individuals can rise above desires, perform their duties with detachment, and find lasting inner peace. True fulfillment does not lie in satisfying endless cravings but in realizing that ultimate joy comes from within.

Relevance in Modern Life

The dilemma of duty versus desire is not confined to the battlefield of Kurukshetra; it manifests in everyday life. Professionals, leaders, and individuals often face situations where personal emotions conflict with ethical obligations. Krishna's teachings encourage individuals to act with integrity, devotion, and detachment from materialistic outcomes.

In the modern world, ambition and personal gain often overshadow ethical considerations. The pursuit of wealth, status, and power can sometimes lead individuals to compromise their values. However, the wisdom of the Bhagavad Gita reminds us to focus on righteous action rather than the rewards it may bring. It calls for a life of selfless service, inner stability, and unwavering commitment to one's responsibilities.

Krishna's principle of **Nishkama Karma (selfless action)** is highly relevant in today's corporate and professional world. Many professionals experience stress and dissatisfaction because they focus too much on promotions, salaries, or recognition rather than on the quality of their work. By shifting their mindset to performing duties sincerely without attachment to outcomes, individuals can find deeper satisfaction and mental peace.

Similarly, **Krishna's emphasis on self-discipline and detachment** can help individuals deal with personal and professional challenges. In an age of instant gratification and consumerism, people often chase short-term pleasures—whether through social media validation, material possessions, or temporary pleasures—without realizing the emptiness they bring. Practicing restraint and mindfulness allows individuals to lead more balanced and fulfilling lives.

Furthermore, **Krishna's call for equanimity** can help individuals navigate setbacks and failures with resilience. Modern life is full of uncertainties—economic fluctuations, job losses, personal failures—but maintaining inner stability helps one rise above disappointments. Accepting both success and failure with a steady mind leads to greater emotional well-being.

Krishna's teachings also have implications for **leadership and decision-making**. Leaders often struggle with difficult choices that require them to balance personal interests with the greater good. By applying the principles of detachment and righteousness, leaders can make ethical decisions that benefit society rather than serving their selfish motives.

In personal relationships, Krishna's guidance on **detachment and unconditional love** can lead to healthier interactions. Instead of forming attachments based on expectations, individuals can cultivate selfless relationships grounded in mutual respect and understanding. This reduces conflicts and fosters harmony.

Ultimately, Krishna's teachings are timeless, offering solutions to both ancient and modern dilemmas. Whether in career, relationships, or personal growth, the wisdom of the Gita provides a roadmap to a more meaningful and fulfilling life. By integrating these principles, individuals can rise above desires, perform their duties with sincerity, and achieve a state of true contentment and peace.

Conclusion

The dialogue between Krishna and Arjuna in the Bhagavad Gita stands as a testament to the eternal struggle between duty and desire. By following Krishna's teachings, one can navigate life's challenges with wisdom, discipline, and selflessness. Arjuna's journey from doubt to determination serves as an inspiration for all who seek to overcome internal conflicts and walk the path of righteousness.

3 Practical applications of *Dharma* in modern life

Introduction

Dharma, a profound and multi-dimensional concept, has been an integral part of human civilization for centuries. Rooted in ancient Indian philosophy, Dharma represents righteousness, duty, ethics, and the moral order that sustains life. While often associated with religion, its essence transcends religious boundaries and applies to every aspect of life. In today's fast-paced and materialistic world, the relevance of Dharma is more crucial than ever. This document explores the practical applications of Dharma in modern life, demonstrating how its principles can guide individuals towards a balanced, ethical, and fulfilling existence.

Dharma in Personal Life

Self-Discipline and Self-Improvement

One of the core tenets of Dharma is self-discipline. Practicing Dharma in personal life means adhering to ethical principles, maintaining integrity, and striving for self-improvement. It encourages individuals to cultivate virtues such as honesty, patience, humility, and perseverance. These values help in building a strong character, leading to a more purposeful and fulfilling life.

Maintaining Balance and Inner Peace

Dharma teaches that life should be lived in balance. Excessive indulgence in material pleasures or extreme asceticism can both lead to suffering. By practicing moderation, one can achieve inner peace and contentment. This balance extends to all aspects of life, including work, relationships, and personal well-being.

Role of Meditation, Yoga, and Mindfulness

Ancient practices such as meditation and yoga are deeply connected to Dharma. They help individuals attain self-awareness, reduce stress, and enhance mental clarity. Mindfulness, or being present in the moment, is another practical application that fosters patience, resilience, and a sense of gratitude.

Overcoming Stress and Challenges with Dharma

Modern life is filled with challenges, from financial struggles to emotional turmoil. The principles of Dharma offer a guiding light during difficult times. By practicing acceptance, detachment from outcomes, and perseverance, individuals can navigate challenges with a calm and composed mind.

Dharma in Family and Society

Establishing Strong Family Values

Family is the foundation of society, and Dharma emphasizes the importance of strong familial bonds. Respecting elders, caring for parents, nurturing children with good values, and maintaining harmony within the family are all part of Dharma in action.

Compassion, Love, and Empathy in Relationships

Interpersonal relationships thrive on trust, love, and compassion. Practicing Dharma means treating others with kindness, understanding their perspectives, and acting selflessly. This not only strengthens personal bonds but also contributes to a more harmonious society.

Dharma as a Foundation for Social Harmony

A society built on Dharma is just, fair, and inclusive. By upholding ethical principles, people can create a culture of trust and cooperation. Acts of charity, community service, and helping those in need reflect the essence of Dharma in social life.

Resolving Conflicts Through Dharma-Based Principles

Disputes and conflicts are inevitable in human interactions. Dharma provides a framework for resolving conflicts through dialogue, understanding, and justice. Instead of resorting to aggression or deceit, individuals can seek peaceful and fair resolutions based on ethical considerations.

Dharma in Work and Business

Ethics and Integrity in the Workplace

The application of Dharma in professional life promotes honesty, responsibility, and ethical decision-making. A work environment guided by Dharma fosters trust, loyalty, and a sense of purpose among employees and employers alike.

Leadership and Karma Yoga Principles

Leadership based on Dharma involves leading by example, prioritizing the well-being of others, and making fair decisions. The principle of Karma Yoga, which emphasizes selfless action without attachment to outcomes, is highly relevant in modern leadership.

Balancing Material Success with Spiritual Values

While material success is important, it should not come at the cost of ethics and human values. Dharma teaches that wealth should be earned through honest means and used for the betterment of society. Striking a balance between ambition and moral responsibility ensures a more fulfilling career.

Responsible Decision-Making and Sustainable Business

Businesses guided by Dharma prioritize sustainability, ethical labor practices, and social responsibility. Companies that follow Dharma contribute positively to society, ensuring long-term success and goodwill.

Dharma in Governance and Leadership

Ancient Wisdom for Modern Leadership

Dharma-based governance emphasizes justice, fairness, and the well-being of all citizens. Ancient leaders like Ashoka and Vikramaditya exemplified righteous leadership by prioritizing ethical governance.

The Concept of "Dharma Rajya" (Righteous Governance)

A government that follows Dharma ensures social justice, economic stability, and equal opportunities for all. It works towards the welfare of people rather than personal gains or power struggles.

Justice, Fairness, and Social Welfare

A society governed by Dharma upholds justice and fairness, ensuring that laws are applied equally to all. Social welfare programs, protection of human rights, and inclusive policies are practical implementations of Dharma in governance.

Fighting Corruption Through Dharma

Corruption erodes the moral fabric of society. A Dharma-centered approach in politics and administration promotes transparency, accountability, and honesty, reducing the prevalence of unethical practices.

Dharma in Education and Learning

Importance of Value-Based Education

Education should go beyond academic knowledge to include ethical and moral values. Teaching students about Dharma encourages them to become responsible, compassionate, and ethical individuals.

Teaching Dharma in Schools and Universities

Incorporating Dharma-based teachings in educational institutions helps nurture well-rounded individuals who contribute positively to society. Lessons on honesty, duty, and responsibility shape future leaders and citizens.

Role of Teachers and Students in Upholding Dharma

Teachers play a vital role in imparting ethical values, while students must embrace these principles in their lives. Mutual respect, curiosity, and a commitment to truth are key aspects of Dharma in education.

Encouraging Critical Thinking with Moral Responsibility

Education should encourage critical thinking while ensuring that knowledge is used ethically. Dharma-based education promotes intellectual growth along with moral consciousness.

Dharma and Technology

Ethical Use of Technology

With rapid technological advancements, ethical concerns have emerged. Dharma encourages the responsible use of technology for the betterment of humanity rather than for exploitation or harm.

Impact of Social Media on Moral Values

Social media can spread positivity or misinformation. Practicing Dharma means using these platforms responsibly, promoting truth, and avoiding harmful or divisive content.

Artificial Intelligence and Ethical Dilemmas

As AI continues to evolve, ethical considerations become crucial. Dharma-based principles can guide decision-making in AI development, ensuring fairness and accountability.

How Dharma Can Guide the Digital Revolution

The integration of Dharma into the digital world promotes innovation while maintaining ethical boundaries. It ensures that technological progress aligns with human well-being and moral integrity.

Dharma and Environmental Responsibility

Sustainable Living and Ecological Consciousness

Dharma teaches respect for nature. Sustainable living, conservation efforts, and responsible consumption reflect Dharma in action.

Traditional Wisdom for Environmental Protection

Ancient practices such as afforestation, water conservation, and biodiversity preservation align with modern sustainability goals.

Responsibilities Towards Nature and Future Generations

Practicing Dharma means protecting the environment for future generations. Conscious efforts to reduce pollution and adopt eco-friendly habits are essential applications.

Practical Solutions for a Greener World

Using renewable energy, minimizing waste, and supporting green initiatives are ways to incorporate Dharma into environmental efforts.

Conclusion

Dharma is a timeless and universal principle that holds immense relevance in modern life. By incorporating its teachings into personal conduct, professional ethics, governance, education, technology, and environmental responsibility, individuals and societies can create a just, harmonious, and sustainable world. Living by Dharma ensures that progress does not come at the cost of values but is instead guided by them, leading to a fulfilling and meaningful existence.

Chapter 03: Yoga in the Bhagavad Gita: Paths to Liberation

The Bhagavad Gita presents yoga as a spiritual discipline that leads to liberation (moksha). It describes different paths of yoga, each suited to an individual's nature, temperament, and level of understanding. The four primary paths of yoga mentioned in the Gita are:

1 Karma Yoga (The Path of Action) in the Bhagavad Gita

Introduction

Karma Yoga, or the path of action, is one of the central teachings of the Bhagavad Gita. It emphasizes performing one's duty with dedication while remaining unattached to the results. This approach aligns with the philosophy of selfless service and fosters spiritual growth. In the Bhagavad Gita, Lord Krishna explains Karma Yoga to Arjuna, guiding him to act with righteousness (dharma) without attachment to success or failure.

Definition of Karma Yoga

Karma Yoga is derived from two Sanskrit words: **Karma** (action) and **Yoga** (union or discipline). It is the practice of performing actions selflessly, offering the results to the Divine. According to Lord Krishna in the Bhagavad Gita:

"Karmanyevadhikaraste mā phaleṣu kadācana"
(Bhagavad Gita 2.47)

This verse encapsulates the essence of Karma Yoga, emphasizing duty over results and selfless action over selfish motives.

Principles of Karma Yoga

1. **Performing Duty (Dharma):** Each individual has a duty (swadharma) according to their role in society. Karma Yoga encourages fulfilling responsibilities with sincerity and dedication.

2. **Detachment from Results:** Actions should be performed without attachment to their outcomes, whether positive or negative.

3. **Selfless Service (Seva):** Serving others without expecting rewards leads to inner peace and spiritual growth.

4. **Equanimity (Samatva):** A Karma Yogi maintains a balanced mind in success and failure, pleasure and pain.

5. **Offering to the Divine:** Actions should be dedicated to the Supreme Being, considering them as an offering to God.

6. **Avoidance of Ego and Desire:** True Karma Yoga requires overcoming selfish desires and acting without egoistic attachment.

Karma Yoga in the Bhagavad Gita

Lord Krishna elaborates on Karma Yoga throughout the Bhagavad Gita, providing insights into how actions should be performed.

Karma and Duty (Swadharma)

Krishna tells Arjuna:

> **"Shreyan swadharmo vigunah paradharmat svanushthitat"** *(Bhagavad Gita 3.35)*

(It is better to perform one's own duty, even imperfectly, than to perform another's duty perfectly.)

This highlights the importance of focusing on one's responsibilities rather than comparing oneself to others.

Renunciation through Action

Karma Yoga does not mean inactivity but renouncing the attachment to results. Krishna says:

> **"Tyaktvā karmaphalāsaṅgaṁ nitya-tṛpto nirāśrayaḥ"** *(Bhagavad Gita 4.20)*

(One who abandons attachment to results and remains content in the self is truly free.)

A Karma Yogi works with dedication but is not bound by expectations of gain or loss.

Sacrificial Nature of Work

Krishna teaches that all work should be seen as a sacrifice (yajna):

"Yajñārthāt karmaṇo'nyatra loko'yaṁ karma-bandhanaḥ" *(Bhagavad Gita 3.9)*

(Work done as a sacrifice for the Divine frees one from bondage; work done for selfish motives binds the soul.)

Thus, selfless service liberates the soul, whereas ego-driven work leads to attachment and suffering.

Types of Actions in Karma Yoga

1. **Nishkama Karma (Selfless Action):** Performing duty without expecting results.

2. **Sakama Karma (Selfish Action):** Acting with a desire for personal gain.

3. **Akarma (Inaction):** Misinterpretation of detachment leading to inaction, which Krishna warns against.

The highest form of Karma Yoga is **Nishkama Karma**, where one performs duties as a service to God, without craving rewards.

Benefits of Practicing Karma Yoga

1. **Inner Peace:** Detachment from results leads to mental peace and reduces anxiety.

2. **Spiritual Growth:** Selfless action purifies the mind and prepares it for higher spiritual realization.

3. **Freedom from Bondage:** Actions performed without selfish motives do not create karmic entanglements.

4. **Improved Relationships:** A Karma Yogi works for the welfare of others, fostering love and harmony.

5. **Greater Efficiency:** A detached yet dedicated mindset improves focus and efficiency.

Real-Life Application of Karma Yoga

1. **Workplace Ethics:** Executing professional responsibilities with dedication while staying detached from promotions or monetary gains.

2. **Social Service:** Engaging in charity, community work, and selfless service without expecting recognition.

3. **Personal Life:** Fulfilling family responsibilities with love and duty rather than material expectations.

4. **Education:** Studying diligently without worrying solely about exam results.

5. **Leadership:** True leaders work for collective well-being rather than personal power.

Misconceptions About Karma Yoga

1. **It Means Avoiding Rewards:** Karma Yoga does not prohibit receiving rewards but teaches detachment from them.

2. **It Advocates Passivity:** It encourages dynamic action, not passivity or laziness.

3. **It is Only for Saints:** It is a practical path for everyone, applicable in daily life.

Comparison with Other Yogic Paths

Aspect	Karma Yoga (Action)	Bhakti Yoga (Devotion)	Jnana Yoga (Knowledge)	Dhyana Yoga (Meditation)
Focus	Selfless service	Love for God	Wisdom and inquiry	Meditation & mindfulness
Goal	Liberation through duty	Union through devotion	Self-realization	Mind control and enlightenment
Key Practice	Action without attachment	Worship and surrender	Study and contemplation	Meditation and concentration

Conclusion

Karma Yoga is a profound path that teaches selfless action, discipline, and devotion to duty. By following this path, one attains inner peace and spiritual liberation. As Krishna reassures Arjuna:

"Yogah karmasu kaushalam" *(Bhagavad Gita 2.50)*

(Yoga is skill in action.)

Thus, Karma Yoga transforms every action into a means of spiritual evolution, leading ultimately to liberation (moksha). It remains one of the most practical and impactful paths to self-realization in the modern world.

2 Bhakti Yoga (The Path of Devotion) in the Bhagavad Gita

Introduction

Bhakti Yoga, or the path of devotion, is one of the central teachings of the Bhagavad Gita. It emphasizes loving devotion to God as the ultimate means of attaining spiritual liberation (moksha). Lord Krishna presents Bhakti Yoga as the simplest and most accessible path, one that transcends intellectual complexity and rigorous austerities. It is based on surrender, love, and faith in the Divine.

Definition of Bhakti Yoga

The word "Bhakti" comes from the Sanskrit root *bhaj*, which means "to worship, to adore, or to love with devotion." Bhakti Yoga, therefore, is the yoga of love and surrender to God. As Krishna declares in the Bhagavad Gita:

"Bhaktyā mām abhijānāti yāvān yaś cāsmi tattvataḥ" *(Bhagavad Gita 18.55)*

(Only through devotion can one truly know Me as I am.)

This verse highlights that devotion is the key to realizing the true nature of the Divine.

Principles of Bhakti Yoga

1. **Loving Devotion:** The core of Bhakti Yoga is love for God, expressed through prayer, chanting, and worship.

2. **Surrender (Sharanagati):** A devotee surrenders completely to the Divine, trusting in divine will.

3. **Selflessness:** True Bhakti is unconditional, expecting nothing in return.

4. **Constant Remembrance (Smarana):** A Bhakti Yogi keeps the Divine in their thoughts at all times.

5. **Service (Seva):** Devotion is expressed through selfless service to humanity and all living beings.

6. **Faith (Shraddha):** Absolute faith in God and His grace is essential.

Bhakti Yoga in the Bhagavad Gita

Lord Krishna explains Bhakti Yoga in several chapters, particularly in **Chapter 9 (The Most Confidential Knowledge)** and **Chapter 12 (The Yoga of Devotion).**

Exclusive Devotion to God

Krishna assures devotees:

"Ananyāś cintayanto māṁ ye janāḥ paryupāsate"
(Bhagavad Gita 9.22)

(To those who are devoted to Me alone, I provide what they need and preserve what they have.)

This verse emphasizes that God takes personal responsibility for His devotees' well-being.

The Qualities of a True Devotee

In Chapter 12, Krishna describes the characteristics of an ideal devotee:

"Adveṣṭā sarva-bhūtānāṁ maitraḥ karuṇa eva ca"
(Bhagavad Gita 12.13-14)

(A devotee is free from hatred, friendly, compassionate, forgiving, and content.)

Thus, Bhakti Yoga is not just about rituals; it transforms one's character.

Different Forms of Bhakti

1. **Sakama Bhakti (Devotional Service with Desire):** Devotion with personal desires or wishes.

2. **Nishkama Bhakti (Selfless Devotion):** Unconditional love for God, expecting nothing in return.

3. **Apara Bhakti (Lower Devotion):** Ritualistic devotion without deep understanding.

4. **Para Bhakti (Higher Devotion):** Deep, unwavering love and surrender to God.

Types of Devotees

Krishna classifies devotees into four types:

1. **Arta (The Distressed):** Those who turn to God in times of suffering.

2. **Jijnasu (The Seeker of Knowledge):** Those who seek wisdom about God.

3. **Artharthi (The Seeker of Wealth):** Those who pray for material gains.

4. **Jnani (The Wise Devotee):** Those who worship God with pure knowledge and selflessness.

Among them, Krishna says:

"Vāsudevaḥ sarvam iti sa mahātmā su-durlabhaḥ"
(Bhagavad Gita 7.19)

(The wise one who realizes that God is everything is very rare.)

Nine Forms of Bhakti (Navadha Bhakti)

According to Hindu tradition, Bhakti Yoga manifests in nine forms:

1. **Shravana:** Listening to divine stories and scriptures.

2. **Kirtana:** Singing devotional songs.

3. **Smarana:** Remembering God's name and glories.

4. **Pada-sevana:** Serving the feet of the Divine.

5. **Archana:** Ritualistic worship and offerings.

6. **Vandana:** Prayer and prostration before the Divine.

7. **Dasya:** Serving God as a servant.

8. **Sakhya:** Developing friendship with the Divine.

9. **Atma-nivedana:** Complete surrender of the self.

Benefits of Bhakti Yoga

1. **Inner Peace:** Devotion dissolves worries and brings mental tranquility.

2. **Freedom from Ego:** Love for God removes self-centeredness and pride.

3. **Emotional Strength:** Devotees find comfort and resilience in challenging times.

4. **Spiritual Liberation:** Bhakti leads to ultimate freedom from the cycle of birth and death.

5. **Unconditional Joy:** Devotees experience bliss through divine connection.

Real-Life Application of Bhakti Yoga

1. **Chanting God's Name:** Regular recitation of mantras or prayers, such as Hare Krishna Mahamantra.

2. **Community Service:** Helping the poor, feeding the hungry as an act of devotion.

3. **Meditation on the Divine:** Contemplating God's form and qualities.

4. **Engaging in Worship:** Attending temples, festivals, and satsangs.

5. **Expressing Gratitude:** Acknowledging everything as God's blessing.

Misconceptions About Bhakti Yoga

1. **It is only for the emotionally driven:** Bhakti is for all, including intellectuals and scholars.

2. **It is a passive path:** True Bhakti involves active service and effort.

3. **It requires renunciation:** Bhakti can be practiced by householders as well.

4. **It is limited to rituals:** Bhakti is more about inner transformation than external rituals.

Comparison with Other Yogic Paths

Aspect	Bhakti Yoga (Devotion)	Karma Yoga (Action)	Jnana Yoga (Knowledge)	Dhyana Yoga (Meditation)
Focus	Love for God	Selfless service	Wisdom & inquiry	Mind control
Goal	Union through surrender	Liberation through duty	Self-realization	Enlightenment
Key Practice	Chanting, worship	Performing duty	Studying scriptures	Deep meditation

Conclusion

Bhakti Yoga is the simplest and most joyful path to God. It requires no intellectual expertise, rigorous discipline, or ascetic hardships—only pure, loving surrender. As Krishna assures:

"Patraṁ puṣpaṁ phalaṁ toyaṁ yo me bhaktyā prayacchati" *(Bhagavad Gita 9.26)*

(Whoever offers Me a leaf, a flower, fruit, or water with devotion, I accept it.)

Thus, Bhakti Yoga makes divine connection accessible to all. Love, surrender, and devotion become the bridge to the Supreme, leading the devotee to eternal bliss and liberation.

3 Jnana Yoga (The Path of Knowledge) in the Bhagavad Gita

Introduction

Jnana Yoga, or the path of knowledge, is one of the key spiritual paths described in the Bhagavad Gita. It is the pursuit of wisdom and self-realization through deep inquiry, self-reflection, and the understanding of ultimate truth (Brahman). Jnana Yoga is considered the most direct yet the most challenging path, as it requires intense mental discipline and detachment from worldly illusions.

Definition of Jnana Yoga

The word "Jnana" means "knowledge" or "wisdom," particularly the higher knowledge of the self (*Atman*) and its unity with the ultimate reality (*Brahman*). Lord Krishna explains that true knowledge is not merely intellectual learning but direct realization of the self:

"Neha nānāsti kiñcana" (*Chandogya Upanishad 6.2.1*)

(There is no diversity here; everything is one.)

In the Bhagavad Gita, Krishna states:

"Jñānena tu tad ajñānaṁ yeṣāṁ nāśitam ātmanaḥ"
(Bhagavad Gita 5.16)

(For those whose ignorance is destroyed by knowledge, the Supreme Self shines like the sun.)

This emphasizes that self-knowledge leads to liberation (*moksha*).

Principles of Jnana Yoga

1. **Self-Inquiry (Vichara):** Questioning one's identity and the nature of existence.

2. **Detachment (Vairagya):** Renouncing attachment to material pleasures.

3. **Discrimination (Viveka):** Distinguishing the real (eternal) from the unreal (temporary).

4. **Renunciation (Sannyasa):** Letting go of ego and false identifications.

5. **Meditation (Dhyana):** Deep contemplation on the self and the divine.

6. **Inner Purity (Shuddhi):** Cultivating a pure mind free from desires and distractions.

Jnana Yoga in the Bhagavad Gita

Jnana Yoga is primarily discussed in **Chapters 4, 7, 9, and 13** of the Bhagavad Gita.

The Knowledge of the Self (Atman)

Krishna teaches Arjuna that the self is eternal and beyond birth and death:

"Na jāyate mriyate vā kadācin" *(Bhagavad Gita 2.20)*

(The soul is never born, nor does it ever die.)

This understanding frees one from fear and attachment.

Overcoming Ignorance (Avidya)

Krishna describes ignorance as the root of suffering:

"Avidyāyām antare vartamānāḥ" *(Bhagavad Gita 4.39)*

(Those who live in ignorance remain bound to the cycle of birth and death.)

Jnana Yoga removes this ignorance, leading to enlightenment.

The Supreme Knowledge (Brahma Jnana)

Krishna explains:

"Brahma-bhūtaḥ prasannātmā na śocati na kāṅkṣati" *(Bhagavad Gita 18.54)*

(One who realizes Brahman is beyond sorrow and desire.)

This realization leads to true peace and liberation.

Steps to Attain Jnana Yoga

The Bhagavad Gita outlines a structured approach:

1. **Listening (Shravana):** Studying scriptures and teachings from enlightened masters.

2. **Reflection (Manana):** Contemplating and analyzing the teachings.

3. **Meditation (Nididhyasana):** Deep meditation to realize the truth.

4. **Self-Realization (Atma Jnana):** Experiencing oneness with Brahman.

Fourfold Qualifications (Sadhana Chatushtaya)

To progress in Jnana Yoga, one must develop:

1. **Discrimination (Viveka):** Distinguishing eternal from non-eternal.

2. **Detachment (Vairagya):** Letting go of worldly attachments.

3. **Six Virtues (Shamadi Shatka Sampatti):** Self-discipline, patience, faith, etc.

4. **Intense Desire for Liberation (Mumukshutva):** A burning aspiration for spiritual freedom.

The Role of Guru in Jnana Yoga

Krishna emphasizes the importance of a guru:

"Tad viddhi praṇipātena paripraśnena sevayā"
(Bhagavad Gita 4.34)

(Approach a realized master with humility and service to gain wisdom.)

A guru helps the seeker navigate spiritual challenges.

Difference Between Jnana Yoga and Other Yogic Paths

Aspect	Jnana Yoga (Knowledge)	Bhakti Yoga (Devotion)	Karma Yoga (Action)	Dhyana Yoga (Meditation)
Focus	Self-inquiry & wisdom	Love for God	Selfless service	Mind control
Goal	Self-realization	Union through surrender	Liberation through duty	Enlightenment
Key Practice	Study, reflection	Prayer, worship	Action with detachment	Deep meditation

Challenges of Jnana Yoga

1. **Intellectual Arrogance:** Over-reliance on logic can hinder true experience.

2. **Detachment Difficulties:** Letting go of ego and attachments is challenging.

3. **Lack of Emotional Connection:** Unlike Bhakti Yoga, Jnana Yoga can feel dry if not balanced.

4. **Solitude Requirement:** Deep contemplation often requires solitude, which may not be practical for everyone.

Real-Life Application of Jnana Yoga

1. **Self-Inquiry:** Asking "Who am I?" to explore one's true identity.

2. **Philosophical Reflection:** Studying Vedantic texts like the Upanishads.

3. **Mindfulness Practices:** Observing thoughts without attachment.

4. **Living with Detachment:** Engaging in the world without being bound by it.

5. **Meditative Contemplation:** Spending time in deep thought on life's ultimate purpose.

Misconceptions About Jnana Yoga

1. **It is only for intellectuals:** Jnana Yoga is for sincere seekers, not just scholars.

2. **It ignores emotions:** Though based on knowledge, it leads to profound inner peace.

3. **It requires renouncing the world:** One can practice Jnana Yoga while living a normal life.

Conclusion

Jnana Yoga is the path of knowledge that leads to self-realization and liberation. It requires deep contemplation, inner purity, and detachment from illusions. As Krishna assures:

"Jñānavān māṁ prapadyate vāsudevaḥ sarvam iti"
(Bhagavad Gita 7.19)

(The wise one realizes that Vasudeva (God) is everything and surrenders to Him.)

Ultimately, Jnana Yoga unveils the eternal truth: that the individual self (*Atman*) and the universal reality (*Brahman*) are one. Through this realization, the seeker attains ultimate freedom and bliss.

4 Dhyana Yoga (The Path of Meditation) in the Bhagavad Gita

Introduction

Dhyana Yoga, or the path of meditation, is a crucial spiritual discipline described in the Bhagavad Gita. It focuses on attaining self-realization and union with the divine through deep concentration and mindfulness. Dhyana Yoga teaches the practitioner to control the mind, withdraw from distractions, and meditate upon the Supreme Reality to achieve inner peace and liberation (*moksha*).

Definition of Dhyana Yoga

The word "Dhyana" means "meditation" or "contemplation." It is the process of focusing the mind on a single point of awareness, leading to the ultimate realization of the self (*Atman*). In the Bhagavad Gita, Lord Krishna explains:

"Yoginām api sarveṣāṁ mad-gatenāntar-ātmanā, śraddhāvān bhajate yo māṁ sa me yuktatamo mataḥ" *(Bhagavad Gita 6.47)*

(Among all yogis, the one who meditates upon Me with faith and devotion is the highest.)

This verse establishes meditation as a supreme spiritual practice.

Principles of Dhyana Yoga

1. **Mind Control (Chitta Vritti Nirodha):** Regulating the fluctuations of the mind.

2. **Detachment (Vairagya):** Renouncing material distractions.

3. **Concentration (Dharana):** Fixing attention on a single point.

4. **Meditation (Dhyana):** Deep, uninterrupted contemplation.

5. **Absorption (Samadhi):** Union with the divine consciousness.

Dhyana Yoga in the Bhagavad Gita

Dhyana Yoga is elaborated in **Chapter 6** of the Bhagavad Gita, titled *The Yoga of Meditation.*

Preparation for Meditation

Krishna outlines the ideal conditions for meditation:

> **"Shuchau deshe pratishthāpya sthiram āsanam ātmanaḥ"** *(Bhagavad Gita 6.11)*

> *(One should sit in a clean place, on a stable seat, and focus the mind.)*

The setting should be serene, undisturbed, and conducive to meditation.

The Correct Posture and Focus

Krishna advises:

> **"Samam kāya-śiro-grīvaṁ dhārayann acalaṁ sthiraḥ"** *(Bhagavad Gita 6.13)*

> *(One should hold the body, head, and neck straight and focus on the divine.)*

A steady posture is essential to maintain concentration and inner stillness.

Controlling Desires and Thoughts

Krishna emphasizes self-restraint:

"Yuktāhāra-vihārasya yukta-ceṣṭasya karmasu"
(Bhagavad Gita 6.16)

(One must balance food, sleep, and actions to achieve success in meditation.)

Excess indulgence or extreme austerity disturbs the mind.

The State of a True Yogi

Krishna describes an enlightened meditator:

"Yogi yuñjīta satatam ātmānaṁ rahasi sthitaḥ"
(Bhagavad Gita 6.10)

(A yogi should always meditate in solitude, free from distractions.)

A true yogi is detached from worldly possessions and immersed in divine contemplation.

Steps to Attain Dhyana Yoga

The Bhagavad Gita provides a structured path:

1. **Discipline (Yama & Niyama):** Ethical conduct and self-discipline.

2. **Posture (Asana):** Maintaining a steady and comfortable seat.

3. **Breath Control (Pranayama):** Regulating the breath to calm the mind.

4. **Withdrawal of Senses (Pratyahara):** Detaching from external distractions.

5. **Concentration (Dharana):** Focusing the mind on a single thought.

6. **Meditation (Dhyana):** Deep, unbroken contemplation.

7. **Absorption (Samadhi):** Merging with the infinite consciousness.

Difference Between Dhyana Yoga and Other Yogic Paths

Aspect	Dhyana Yoga (Meditation)	Jnana Yoga (Knowledge)	Bhakti Yoga (Devotion)	Karma Yoga (Action)
Focus	Mind control & meditation	Self-inquiry & wisdom	Love for God	Selfless service
Goal	Union through stillness	Realization through knowledge	Liberation through surrender	Liberation through duty
Key Practice	Meditation & breath control	Study, reflection	Prayer, worship	Detached action

Challenges of Dhyana Yoga

1. **Restlessness of the Mind:** Thoughts constantly arise, making focus difficult.

2. **Lack of Patience:** Progress in meditation requires long-term dedication.

3. **Worldly Distractions:** Modern life presents many obstacles to deep meditation.

4. **Inconsistent Practice:** Discipline is necessary for steady progress.

5. **Doubts and Uncertainty:** A seeker may struggle with self-doubt.

Krishna's Assurance on Meditation

Krishna reassures Arjuna:

"Nātra saṁśayaḥ" *(Bhagavad Gita 6.40)*

(No effort on this path is ever wasted; even a little progress leads to liberation.)

This encourages practitioners to continue meditation despite difficulties.

The Role of a Guru in Dhyana Yoga

A spiritual teacher (*guru*) guides the seeker in meditation. Krishna advises:

"Tad viddhi praṇipātena paripraśnena sevayā"
(Bhagavad Gita 4.34)

(Approach a realized master with humility to gain true wisdom.)

A guru helps in overcoming mental obstacles and deepening meditation.

Practical Application of Dhyana Yoga

1. **Daily Meditation:** Setting aside time for focused meditation.

2. **Breath Awareness:** Using conscious breathing techniques.

3. **Mindfulness in Action:** Maintaining awareness throughout daily activities.

4. **Chanting Mantras:** Repeating sacred sounds to aid concentration.

5. **Detachment from Materialism:** Reducing unnecessary desires and distractions.

Misconceptions About Dhyana Yoga

1. **It is only for monks:** Meditation can be practiced by anyone, regardless of lifestyle.

2. **It requires long hours:** Even short meditation sessions are beneficial.

3. **It guarantees instant peace:** Meditation requires patience and effort.

4. **It is separate from daily life:** True meditation extends into every moment of living.

Conclusion

Dhyana Yoga is the path of meditation that leads to self-realization and spiritual enlightenment. Through concentration, discipline, and devotion, one can transcend the distractions of the mind and attain union with the divine. As Krishna declares:

"Yoginām api sarveṣāṁ mad-gatenāntar-ātmanā"
(Bhagavad Gita 6.47)

(Among all yogis, the one who meditates upon Me with faith and devotion is the highest.)

Thus, Dhyana Yoga is not just a practice but a way of life that leads to ultimate freedom and bliss.

Chapter 04: The Nature of the Self: Atman and Brahman

Introduction

The concept of the self has been a central theme in Indian philosophy for centuries. Hindu thought, particularly as expressed in the Upanishads, distinguishes between the individual self (*Atman*) and the universal, supreme reality (*Brahman*). This philosophical inquiry seeks to understand the nature of existence, the relationship between the finite and the infinite, and the ultimate goal of human life—liberation (*Moksha*).

The Eternal Soul: Atman

The concept of the self and soul has been a subject of deep philosophical inquiry in various traditions. However, in Hinduism, particularly in the Vedantic and Upanishadic schools of thought, the term *Atman* holds profound significance. Atman refers to the eternal, unchanging essence of an individual, the true self that transcends the physical and mental realms. Unlike the fleeting aspects of personality, identity, and ego, Atman is regarded as pure consciousness, beyond birth and death. This essay delves into the nature of Atman, its philosophical underpinnings, and its implications for human life and spiritual progress.

The Definition and Nature of Atman

Atman is the Sanskrit term for the self or soul, distinct from the body, mind, and emotions. The Upanishads describe Atman as imperishable, infinite, and divine. The

Chandogya Upanishad famously declares, *"Tat Tvam Asi"* (Thou art That), implying that the individual self is not separate from the universal reality. Atman is characterized by *Sat* (existence), *Chit* (consciousness), and *Ananda* (bliss), forming the core of all living beings.

Unlike the physical body, which is subject to decay, and the mind, which fluctuates, Atman remains constant. It is untouched by suffering, change, or dualities such as pleasure and pain. In the Bhagavad Gita, Lord Krishna tells Arjuna:

"The soul is neither born, nor does it die. It has never been brought into being, nor will it cease to be. It is unborn, eternal, permanent, and primeval. It is not slain when the body is slain." (Bhagavad Gita 2:20)

This verse highlights the indestructible nature of Atman and its distinction from the perishable material world.

Atman in the Upanishads

The Upanishads, the philosophical texts of Hinduism, provide extensive discussions on Atman. They explore its nature through metaphors, dialogues, and logical reasoning. The *Brihadaranyaka Upanishad* describes Atman as "neti, neti" (not this, not that), signifying that it is beyond all physical and conceptual limitations.

The *Mandukya Upanishad* presents the concept of the four states of consciousness—waking (*Jagrat*), dreaming (*Swapna*), deep sleep (*Sushupti*), and the transcendental state (*Turiya*). In the Turiya state, one experiences the pure Atman, free from worldly distractions. This state is beyond duality, where the self is realized in its purest form.

The Atman-Brahman Connection

One of the most profound ideas in Vedanta is the relationship between Atman and Brahman. While Atman represents the individual self, Brahman is the ultimate, unchanging reality that pervades the universe. The Advaita Vedanta school, founded by Adi Shankaracharya, asserts that Atman and Brahman are one and the same. This idea is encapsulated in the Mahavakya (great saying): *"Aham Brahmasmi"* (I am Brahman).

According to this philosophy, the realization that one's Atman is not different from Brahman leads to spiritual liberation (*Moksha*). The perception of separateness is due to *Avidya* (ignorance), and overcoming this illusion through self-inquiry (*Jnana Yoga*) leads to enlightenment.

The Journey to Self-Realization

Realizing Atman as one's true nature is the ultimate goal of spiritual life. This realization is not intellectual but experiential. Various paths in Hinduism guide seekers toward this self-awareness:

1. **Jnana Yoga (Path of Knowledge)** – This involves deep inquiry and contemplation on the nature of the self. The seeker questions the reality of the ego and identifies with the pure consciousness beyond.

2. **Bhakti Yoga (Path of Devotion)** – Through devotion to the divine, one cultivates love and

surrender, dissolving the ego and experiencing the unity of Atman and Brahman.

3. **Karma Yoga (Path of Action)** – Performing selfless actions without attachment purifies the mind and leads to self-realization.

4. **Raja Yoga (Path of Meditation)** – Practices like meditation and mindfulness help transcend mental distractions and directly experience Atman.

Atman and Rebirth

The concept of reincarnation (*Samsara*) is closely linked to Atman. Hinduism teaches that Atman is eternal and takes on different bodies across lifetimes based on *Karma* (actions). This cycle continues until Moksha is attained. The *Katha Upanishad* states:

"As a person casts off worn-out clothes and puts on new ones, so does the soul cast off its worn-out bodies and enter into new ones." (Katha Upanishad 2:22)

This metaphor explains how Atman remains unchanged despite the physical transformations it undergoes.

The Role of Atman in Daily Life

Understanding Atman is not just a theoretical exercise but has practical implications. Recognizing that one is not merely the body or mind but an eternal soul changes how one approaches life. It fosters inner peace, resilience, and detachment from materialistic anxieties. This realization also encourages compassion, as one sees the same divine essence in all beings.

Atman is the eternal, indestructible essence of all living beings. It is the foundation of consciousness and the key to spiritual enlightenment. Through self-inquiry, devotion, and righteous action, individuals can transcend ignorance and realize their true nature. The wisdom of Atman, deeply embedded in Hindu philosophy, continues to guide seekers on their path to ultimate liberation and peace.

The Supreme Reality: Brahman

Introduction

Brahman, in Hindu philosophy, is the ultimate, infinite, and unchanging reality that transcends all worldly existence. It is beyond perception, beyond description, and beyond the material realm. Unlike physical objects or mental constructs, Brahman is eternal and all-pervasive, forming the foundation of the entire cosmos. The Upanishads, Bhagavad Gita, and Advaita Vedanta provide profound insights into the nature of Brahman, its relationship with Atman (the individual self), and the path to realizing this ultimate truth.

The Definition and Nature of Brahman

Brahman is often described as *Sat-Chit-Ananda* (Existence, Consciousness, and Bliss). It is not a deity or a personal god but the formless, infinite, and undivided essence of all existence. The Upanishads repeatedly emphasize that Brahman is beyond the grasp of human intellect and cannot be comprehended through sensory perception or logical reasoning alone. Instead, it is realized through deep meditation and self-inquiry.

The Brihadaranyaka Upanishad states:

"Neti, Neti" (Not this, Not that)

This phrase indicates that Brahman cannot be defined by conventional means. It is beyond all attributes (*Nirguna*), yet it manifests within creation (*Saguna*). This paradoxical nature makes Brahman a deeply complex and profound concept.

The Upanishadic Perspective on Brahman

The Upanishads, the foundational texts of Vedanta, offer numerous teachings on Brahman. Some of the key Mahavakyas (great statements) that describe Brahman include:

1. **"Tat Tvam Asi" (Thou Art That)** – Chandogya Upanishad

2. **"Aham Brahmasmi" (I Am Brahman)** – Brihadaranyaka Upanishad

3. **"Sarvam Khalvidam Brahma" (All This Is Brahman)** – Chandogya Upanishad

4. **"Prajnanam Brahma" (Consciousness Is Brahman)** – Aitareya Upanishad

Each of these Mahavakyas conveys the fundamental idea that Brahman and Atman are one. The perceived separation between the individual self and the supreme reality is an illusion (*Maya*), which must be overcome through spiritual wisdom.

Brahman in Advaita Vedanta

Advaita Vedanta, established by Adi Shankaracharya, asserts the non-duality (*Advaita*) of Brahman. It teaches that the world is *Maya* (illusion), and the only reality is Brahman. According to this school of thought, self-realization (*Jnana Yoga*) is the key to Moksha (liberation), where the individual recognizes their unity with Brahman.

Shankaracharya explains:

> *"Brahman alone is real, the world is illusion, and the individual self is not different from Brahman."*

This philosophy negates the idea of separateness and urges seekers to transcend ego-based identity and merge into the infinite consciousness.

The Relationship Between Brahman and Atman

While Brahman is the absolute reality, Atman is the individual self. According to Vedanta, Atman is not different from Brahman but is merely obscured by ignorance (*Avidya*). The realization that Atman and Brahman are one leads to enlightenment. This self-realization is not intellectual but an experiential understanding gained through meditation, self-inquiry, and devotion.

The Bhagavad Gita (Chapter 10:20) states:

> *"I am the Atman, seated in the hearts of all beings."*

This verse highlights that Brahman is not distant or separate but is present within every living being as pure consciousness.

Saguna and Nirguna Brahman

Hindu philosophy distinguishes between two aspects of Brahman:

1. **Nirguna Brahman** – The formless, attribute-less, absolute reality.

2. **Saguna Brahman** – Brahman with attributes, often personified as Ishvara (God).

Devotional traditions such as Vaishnavism and Shaivism emphasize Saguna Brahman, worshiping forms like Vishnu or Shiva as manifestations of the supreme reality. However, Advaita Vedanta maintains that the ultimate truth is Nirguna Brahman, beyond all names and forms.

Brahman and the Concept of Maya

Maya, or illusion, is the veil that obscures the true nature of reality. It creates the appearance of duality, making individuals believe in separateness from Brahman. The world, as perceived by the senses, is transient and ever-changing, while Brahman is eternal and unchanging. Spiritual awakening involves seeing through the illusion of Maya and realizing the oneness of all existence.

The Path to Realizing Brahman

The realization of Brahman requires a disciplined spiritual practice. The main paths to achieving this knowledge include:

1. **Jnana Yoga (Path of Knowledge)** – Inquiry into the nature of the self through scriptural study and meditation.

2. **Bhakti Yoga (Path of Devotion)** – Surrendering to a personal deity, leading to the dissolution of the ego.

3. **Karma Yoga (Path of Action)** – Performing selfless actions without attachment to results.

4. **Raja Yoga (Path of Meditation)** – Achieving inner stillness through meditation and control of the mind.

Each of these paths, though different in approach, ultimately leads to the realization of Brahman.

Brahman in Daily Life

Understanding Brahman is not merely a philosophical exercise; it has profound implications for daily living. When one realizes that all beings are manifestations of the same divine essence, it fosters compassion, humility, and inner peace. Recognizing the transient nature of worldly experiences reduces attachment and suffering, leading to a life of balance and wisdom.

Brahman is the infinite, eternal, and all-pervasive reality that forms the essence of everything. The Upanishads, Vedanta, and Hindu scriptures emphasize that realizing Brahman is the highest goal of human life. By transcending ignorance and recognizing the unity of Atman and Brahman, one attains true liberation (*Moksha*). This profound realization dissolves all illusions and leads to ultimate peace, bliss, and enlightenment.

Transcending the Material World

Introduction

The material world is filled with transient pleasures, desires, and attachments that often lead to suffering and discontent. Spiritual traditions across cultures emphasize the need to transcend materialism to attain a deeper sense of peace, fulfillment, and enlightenment. Hinduism, in particular, provides a detailed philosophical framework for understanding the temporary nature of worldly existence and the pathways to transcend it. The concept of *Maya* (illusion) and the pursuit of spiritual liberation (*Moksha*) serve as guiding principles for seekers who wish to go beyond the material realm and experience the ultimate truth.

This exploration of transcending the material world will cover its philosophical underpinnings, its relevance in different spiritual traditions, and practical approaches to achieving detachment while living a balanced life.

Understanding the Material World: The Concept of Maya

In Hindu philosophy, *Maya* refers to the illusion that veils reality. The world appears to be real, but it is constantly changing and impermanent. The Upanishads describe *Maya* as the force that creates duality and attachment, making individuals believe that their identity is limited to their physical existence.

Adi Shankaracharya, the proponent of Advaita Vedanta, famously stated:

"Brahman alone is real; the world is illusion."

This does not mean that the world does not exist, but rather that it is not the ultimate reality. People mistake the temporary for the eternal, leading to suffering and a cycle of endless desires.

The Material World and the Cycle of Samsara

The material world is closely linked to *Samsara*, the cycle of birth, death, and rebirth. According to Hinduism and Buddhism, beings are trapped in *Samsara* due to their attachment to material existence. Actions (*Karma*) determine one's future births, and the only way to break free from this cycle is through spiritual realization.

The Bhagavad Gita (2:22) explains:

"As a person casts off worn-out garments and wears new ones, so does the soul discard old bodies and take on new ones."

This metaphor illustrates that attachment to the physical world is futile, as everything is temporary. Only through detachment and self-realization can one attain liberation.

Paths to Transcending the Material World

Different philosophical and spiritual traditions offer various approaches to transcendence. Hinduism, Buddhism, and Jainism emphasize renunciation, meditation, and self-inquiry as means to go beyond material existence.

1. Jnana Yoga (Path of Knowledge)

Jnana Yoga involves deep philosophical inquiry to understand the illusory nature of the world and recognize one's true self as *Atman*, which is beyond material limitations. The practice of *Neti, Neti* ("Not this, Not that") helps in identifying what is unreal and focusing on the eternal self.

2. Bhakti Yoga (Path of Devotion)

Devotion to a higher power enables an individual to surrender material attachments and seek fulfillment in divine love. By dedicating thoughts and actions to the divine, one gradually moves beyond ego and materialism.

3. Karma Yoga (Path of Selfless Action)

Performing actions without attachment to outcomes allows one to transcend worldly desires. The Bhagavad Gita (3:19) states:

> *"Therefore, always perform your duty efficiently and without attachment to the results, for by doing work without attachment, one attains the Supreme."*

This path teaches that by working with selflessness, one rises above material concerns.

4. Raja Yoga (Path of Meditation and Mind Control)

Raja Yoga focuses on meditation and self-discipline to detach from material distractions. Practices like *Dhyana* (meditation) and *Samadhi* (absorption in pure consciousness) help in breaking the bonds of material illusion.

Transcending Material Desires and Attachments

Material desires are the primary cause of suffering. The Buddha emphasized that attachment leads to suffering (*Dukkha*) and that liberation (*Nirvana*) comes from eliminating cravings. Hinduism similarly teaches that desire (*Kama*) and greed (*Lobha*) keep individuals bound to the material world.

Some practical ways to cultivate detachment include:

- Practicing mindfulness and awareness of impermanence.

- Engaging in acts of selfless service (*Seva*).

- Living a simple and minimalistic lifestyle.

- Developing gratitude for spiritual growth rather than material gain.

Living in the World Without Being of the World

Transcendence does not mean complete renunciation of the world. Many spiritual teachings encourage balance—engaging with the world while maintaining inner detachment. The Bhagavad Gita (5:10) advises:

"One who performs duties without attachment, surrendering the results to the Supreme, is untouched by sin, just as a lotus leaf remains untouched by water."

This means that a person can fulfill worldly responsibilities without being consumed by materialism.

Transcending the material world is a journey of recognizing the impermanent nature of physical existence and striving for spiritual liberation. By following paths like Jnana Yoga, Bhakti Yoga, Karma Yoga, and Raja Yoga, individuals can rise above material attachments and attain lasting peace. Understanding *Maya*, overcoming desires, and practicing detachment lead to a life of wisdom, balance, and ultimate liberation (*Moksha*).

Death and Rebirth: Understanding Samsara and Moksha

Introduction

The cycle of birth, death, and rebirth—known as *Samsara*—is one of the fundamental concepts in Hindu, Buddhist, and Jain philosophies. It represents the continuous journey of the soul (*Atman*) through various lifetimes, shaped by past actions (*Karma*). Liberation from this cycle, known as *Moksha*, is the ultimate spiritual goal, leading to eternal peace and unity with the supreme reality (*Brahman*).

Understanding *Samsara* and *Moksha* involves exploring the nature of existence, the law of *Karma*, and the spiritual paths that help transcend the cycle of rebirth. This discussion will cover the philosophical underpinnings, religious interpretations, and practical means of achieving liberation.

The Concept of Samsara

Samsara is derived from the Sanskrit root meaning "to flow" or "to wander." It symbolizes the endless cycle of life, death, and rebirth, where the soul takes on different physical forms based on its accumulated *Karma*.

1. The Nature of Samsara

Samsara is often described as a state of suffering and impermanence. The Bhagavad Gita (2:27) states:

"For one who has taken birth, death is certain, and for one who has died, birth is certain."

This highlights the inevitability of rebirth, where life is characterized by temporary pleasures and sorrows. In Hinduism, Samsara is governed by *Maya* (illusion), which creates the false sense of individuality and attachment to worldly experiences.

2. The Role of Karma in Samsara

Karma refers to the law of cause and effect, where actions from past lives influence present circumstances and future rebirths. The Brihadaranyaka Upanishad (4.4.5) explains:

"A person becomes good by good actions and bad by bad actions."

Every thought, word, and deed generate *Karma*, binding the soul to Samsara. The different types of *Karma* include:

- **Sanchita Karma** – Accumulated past actions waiting to bear fruit.

- **Prarabdha Karma** – The portion of past karma influencing the present life.

- **Kriyamana Karma** – Actions performed in the present that shape the future.

Only through selfless action and spiritual discipline can one break free from this cycle.

The Journey of the Soul After Death

Different scriptures provide insights into what happens after death and how the soul transitions between lives.

1. The Garuda Purana's Perspective

The *Garuda Purana* describes the afterlife journey, where the soul experiences *Yama Loka* (the realm of the god of death) before moving toward its next birth. Good deeds lead to *Swarga* (heaven), while negative actions result in *Naraka* (hell). However, both experiences are temporary, and the soul eventually reincarnates.

2. The Bhagavad Gita's View

The Bhagavad Gita (8:6) states:

> *"Whatever state of being one remembers at the time of death, that state he will attain in the next birth."*

This emphasizes the importance of consciousness at the moment of death, suggesting that a spiritually inclined mind leads to a higher birth or even liberation.

3. Buddhist and Jain Perspectives

Buddhism and Jainism also accept Samsara but emphasize slightly different pathways to liberation. Buddhism teaches that ignorance and attachment perpetuate rebirth, while Jainism views *Karma* as a physical substance binding the soul.

The Ultimate Goal: Moksha

Moksha is the liberation from *Samsara*, where the soul transcends material existence and merges with the infinite reality. It is the realization that the self (*Atman*) is not separate from *Brahman*.

1. Characteristics of Moksha

- **Freedom from Karma:** All accumulated Karma is dissolved, ending the cycle of rebirth.

- **Pure Consciousness:** The soul exists in a state of bliss and knowledge.

- **Oneness with Brahman:** According to Advaita Vedanta, Moksha is the realization that *Atman* and *Brahman* are one.

2. Paths to Moksha

Different spiritual traditions offer various means to attain Moksha. These include:

- **Jnana Yoga (Path of Knowledge):** Realizing the illusory nature of the world and recognizing one's divine essence.

- **Bhakti Yoga (Path of Devotion):** Surrendering to God and cultivating divine love.

- **Karma Yoga (Path of Action):** Performing selfless duties without attachment to results.

- **Raja Yoga (Path of Meditation):** Achieving self-control and deep meditation to dissolve ego and ignorance.

Overcoming Attachment and Desire

The greatest obstacles to Moksha are attachment (*Raga*) and ignorance (*Avidya*). The Upanishads emphasize renunciation and detachment as essential steps toward liberation. Practices that aid in overcoming material bondage include:

- **Meditation and mindfulness** to develop awareness of impermanence.

- **Ethical living** to reduce negative karma.

- **Self-inquiry** to detach from ego and worldly identities.

Samsara and Moksha represent the cycle of existence and its ultimate transcendence. While Samsara binds individuals through Karma and desires, Moksha offers freedom and eternal peace. By understanding the impermanent nature of life and following spiritual disciplines, one can break free from the cycle of rebirth and attain self-realization. The journey from death to rebirth, and ultimately to liberation, is the essence of Hindu philosophical thought, guiding seekers toward eternal truth and bliss.

Conclusion

The nature of the self, as understood through Atman and Brahman, provides profound insights into human existence and the spiritual journey. Recognizing Atman as Brahman leads to liberation from the material world and the realization of one's eternal, divine nature. This wisdom, preserved in Hindu philosophy, continues to inspire seekers of truth across the world, guiding them toward self-discovery and ultimate peace.

Chapter 05: Detachment and Equanimity: The Art of Living

Introduction

In the pursuit of a fulfilling and meaningful life, one of the greatest challenges human beings face is maintaining inner peace amidst external chaos. The ancient wisdom of the *Bhagavad Gita* introduces the concept of **Sthitaprajna**, a state of steady wisdom where a person remains unshaken by worldly events, neither elated by success nor disturbed by failure. This state embodies **detachment** and **equanimity**, two essential qualities that help navigate life with clarity and inner stability.

Detachment is often misunderstood as indifference or disengagement from the world, but in reality, it signifies the ability to participate in life without being bound by emotional extremes. Equanimity, on the other hand, is the art of maintaining mental calmness and composure, irrespective of circumstances. Together, these principles offer a roadmap for a balanced and harmonious life.

This essay explores the philosophical foundations of detachment and equanimity, their psychological implications, and practical ways to integrate them into daily life.

1 Sthitaprajna: The State of Steady Wisdom

In the pursuit of a meaningful and fulfilling life, individuals often seek stability amidst the ever-changing external world. The ancient wisdom of the *Bhagavad Gita* introduces the concept of **Sthitaprajna**, a state of steady wisdom where one remains unshaken by worldly events—neither overly joyful in success nor deeply disturbed by failure. This state of being embodies **detachment** and **equanimity**, offering a roadmap for inner stability and self-mastery.

The modern world, filled with distractions, stress, and uncertainty, challenges individuals in maintaining composure. Yet, the teachings of the *Bhagavad Gita* and various psychological insights emphasize that it is possible to cultivate an inner sanctuary of peace, irrespective of external circumstances. This essay explores the philosophical foundations of **Sthitaprajna**, its significance in life, the psychological implications of detachment and equanimity, and practical ways to integrate these principles into daily life.

Understanding Sthitaprajna: A State Beyond Dualities

The word **Sthitaprajna** is derived from two Sanskrit words: *sthita*, meaning 'steady' or 'firm,' and *prajna*, meaning 'wisdom' or 'intellect.' A person who attains this state has unwavering wisdom and remains unaffected by the dualities of life—pleasure and pain, success and failure, praise and criticism.

In Chapter 2 of the *Bhagavad Gita*, Lord Krishna describes the characteristics of a **Sthitaprajna**:

"A person who is not disturbed by sorrow, who does not crave pleasure, who is free from attachment, fear, and

anger, is called a sage of steady wisdom." (Bhagavad Gita 2.56)

A **Sthitaprajna** is not indifferent but deeply aware. The difference lies in their response to situations. They do not react impulsively but rather act with **clarity, awareness, and an unwavering sense of peace**.

The Role of Detachment in Achieving Steady Wisdom

One of the key qualities of a **Sthitaprajna** is detachment—freedom from excessive attachment to desires, emotions, and external outcomes. However, detachment does not mean renunciation of life; rather, it signifies engaging fully in life without becoming entangled in it.

A. The Difference Between Detachment and Indifference

- **Detachment**: Engaging in life with awareness and responsibility while remaining free from emotional turbulence.

- **Indifference**: Apathy or disengagement, leading to a lack of care or involvement in life's duties.

A **Sthitaprajna** practices detachment by accepting life as it comes, without clinging to transient emotions or experiences. This mindset allows one to remain calm, balanced, and wise in all circumstances.

B. Psychological Insights on Detachment

Modern psychology supports the idea that **detachment reduces stress, anxiety, and emotional suffering**.

Cognitive-Behavioral Therapy (CBT) encourages individuals to reframe their thoughts, helping them detach from negative emotions and cultivate a balanced perspective.

Studies have shown that those who practice detachment exhibit:

- **Lower levels of stress and anxiety**

- **Greater emotional stability**

- **Improved decision-making abilities**

- **Enhanced ability to handle life's challenges without overreacting**

Equanimity: The Art of Balance Amidst Chaos

While detachment liberates a person from emotional turmoil, **equanimity** ensures that they maintain a calm and balanced state of mind. Equanimity is the ability to remain **unshaken by external events** while continuing to act with wisdom and purpose.

A. The Benefits of Equanimity

- **Freedom from Emotional Extremes**: Equanimity prevents mood swings caused by success or failure.

- **Better Decision-Making**: A calm mind makes rational and effective choices.

- **Increased Focus and Productivity**: Mental stability enhances concentration.

- **Stronger Relationships**: Equanimity allows for non-reactive communication, leading to healthier relationships.

B. Practices to Cultivate Equanimity

1. **Mindfulness and Meditation**: Observing thoughts without judgment strengthens mental resilience.

2. **Stoic Acceptance of Impermanence**: Recognizing that all experiences are temporary prevents excessive attachment.

3. **Self-Inquiry and Reflection**: Questioning emotional reactions allows for greater self-awareness.

4. **Balanced Living**: Engaging in work, relationships, and self-care in moderation fosters equilibrium.

Overcoming Attachment and Aversion: The Dual Forces of Suffering

In the *Bhagavad Gita*, Lord Krishna explains that human suffering stems from two primary forces:

1. **Attachment (Raga):** The intense desire for things to be a certain way.

2. **Aversion (Dvesha):** The strong dislike or resistance to unpleasant experiences.

A **Sthitaprajna** rises above these forces by understanding the impermanent nature of life.

A. Practical Steps to Reduce Attachment and Aversion

- **Practice Gratitude:** Focusing on the present moment reduces cravings for the future.

- **Accept Life as It Is:** Resisting reality leads to suffering; acceptance brings peace.

- **Focus on Effort, Not Outcome:** Engaging wholeheartedly in actions without fixating on results fosters inner freedom.

Scientific and Neurological Insights on Steady Wisdom

A. Brain Function and Emotional Regulation

Scientific research supports that those who cultivate **equanimity and detachment** exhibit improved mental well-being:

- The **prefrontal cortex** (responsible for rational thinking) strengthens, leading to better emotional control.

- The **amygdala** (associated with fear and stress) becomes less reactive, reducing anxiety.

- Mindfulness practices increase **gray matter density**, enhancing cognitive stability.

These findings indicate that practicing detachment and equanimity rewires the brain for greater resilience.

The Path to Becoming a Sthitaprajna

Achieving the state of **Sthitaprajna** requires conscious effort and self-discipline. Below are steps to cultivate steady wisdom:

A. Shift from Reaction to Response

Instead of reacting impulsively, pause, reflect, and respond with awareness.

B. Let Go of Ego-Driven Desires

Recognize that attachments stem from the ego's need for validation and control.

C. Cultivate Self-Discipline

Regular meditation, introspection, and self-study contribute to emotional mastery.

D. Engage in Detached Action

Act wholeheartedly but without attachment to success or failure.

E. Develop a Higher Perspective

Understanding that life is beyond personal control fosters surrender and peace.

2 Freedom from Attachment and Aversion

The human experience is often characterized by a continuous struggle between attachment and aversion. We cling to what we desire and avoid what we dislike, creating cycles of suffering and discontent. Ancient spiritual traditions, particularly the teachings of the *Bhagavad Gita* and Buddhist philosophy, emphasize the importance of transcending these dualities to attain inner peace and wisdom.

This essay explores the nature of **attachment and aversion**, their psychological and neurological implications, and the practical steps to cultivate freedom from them. It also examines how living beyond these tendencies leads to a life of **equanimity, balance, and true fulfillment**.

Understanding Attachment and Aversion

A. Defining Attachment (Raga) and Aversion (Dvesha)

- **Attachment (Raga):** The tendency to cling to pleasurable experiences, relationships, material possessions, or even ideas and beliefs. It stems from a deep-rooted fear of loss and a craving for security.

- **Aversion (Dvesha):** The resistance to unpleasant experiences, discomfort, failure, criticism, or anything perceived as a threat. It leads to avoidance behaviors, anxiety, and unnecessary suffering.

These dual forces govern most human emotions and decisions, trapping individuals in cycles of temporary joy and inevitable distress.

B. The Illusion of Control

Both attachment and aversion arise from the illusion that we can control external circumstances to maintain happiness and avoid suffering. However, since the external world is **impermanent**, any attempt to hold on to desires or push away discomfort leads to frustration and anxiety.

The *Bhagavad Gita* (2.47) advises:

> *"You have the right to perform your duty, but never to the fruits of your work. Let not the fruits of action be your motive, nor let your attachment be to inaction."*

This teaching highlights the futility of attachment to outcomes and encourages a mindset of **detached engagement**.

Psychological and Neurological Perspectives

A. How the Mind is Conditioned by Attachment and Aversion

From childhood, people are conditioned to seek pleasure and avoid pain. Society reinforces the belief that success, wealth, relationships, and status define happiness, while failure and discomfort should be feared. This conditioning shapes unconscious reactions, leading to stress, anxiety, and dissatisfaction.

B. The Role of the Brain: The Amygdala and Prefrontal Cortex

- The **amygdala**, responsible for processing emotions, plays a key role in attachment and aversion by associating experiences with pleasure or fear.

- The **prefrontal cortex**, which governs rational thinking, can regulate emotional responses, helping individuals cultivate detachment and balance.

Meditation and mindfulness practices strengthen the prefrontal cortex, reducing impulsive reactions driven by attachment or aversion.

The Suffering Caused by Attachment and Aversion

A. The Trap of Desire and Fear

Attachment leads to suffering because it creates **dependency on external circumstances**. When things go as desired, there is a temporary sense of happiness, but when they change (as they inevitably do), suffering follows. Similarly, aversion breeds fear, anxiety, and avoidance, limiting personal growth and freedom.

B. Examples of Suffering Due to Attachment and Aversion

- **Relationships:** Clinging to people for emotional security leads to possessiveness and fear of loss, causing pain when relationships change.

- **Material Possessions:** The pursuit of wealth or luxury creates endless cravings, never leading to true contentment.

- **Social Approval:** Seeking validation from others results in anxiety and a lack of authenticity.

- **Fear of Failure:** Avoiding risks due to the fear of failure prevents learning and self-improvement.

**The Path to Freedom: Cultivating Detachment and
    Equanimity**

A. Understanding the Nature of Impermanence

Recognizing that all experiences, emotions, and
possessions are **temporary** helps in reducing attachment.
The Buddhist concept of **Anicca (Impermanence)**
teaches that nothing in life is permanent, and clinging to
transient things only leads to suffering.

B. Practicing Mindfulness and Awareness

Mindfulness allows individuals to observe their emotions
without identifying with them. By being present and
aware, one can detach from impulsive reactions driven by
attachment or aversion.

C. The Power of Non-Attachment

Non-attachment does not mean indifference but rather
**engaging in life fully while remaining free from
emotional bondage**. This mindset allows individuals to
experience joy without fear and face difficulties without
resistance.

The *Bhagavad Gita* (2.50) states:

*"One who is established in yoga relinquishes both good
and bad karma in this life itself. Therefore, strive for
yoga, which is the art of working skillfully."*

This verse emphasizes acting with wisdom, not for
rewards but as a duty.

Practical Steps to Overcome Attachment and Aversion

A. Cultivating Self-Awareness

- Observe personal tendencies towards attachment and aversion.

- Journal thoughts and emotional triggers.

- Practice self-inquiry: "What am I clinging to? Why does this matter to me?"

B. Practicing Gratitude and Contentment

- Shift focus from what is lacking to what is already present.

- Appreciate life's experiences without clinging to them.

C. Engaging in Detached Action (Nishkama Karma)

- Perform duties sincerely without attachment to outcomes.

- Understand that failure and success are mere experiences, not ultimate truths.

D. Meditation and Reflection

- **Vipassana Meditation:** Observing thoughts and emotions as impermanent sensations.

- **Self-Inquiry:** Questioning attachments and recognizing their transient nature.

E. Developing Compassion and Letting Go

- Compassion for others reduces self-centered attachments.

- Forgiveness releases resentment, which is a form of negative attachment.

Living Beyond Attachment and Aversion: The Ultimate Freedom

Freedom from attachment and aversion leads to a state of **equanimity (Upeksha)**, where one remains **calm, centered, and unshaken** by external circumstances. This inner stability results in:

- **Emotional Resilience:** Ability to handle difficulties without distress.

- **Genuine Happiness:** Joy that is independent of external conditions.

- **Clarity in Decision-Making:** Acting from wisdom rather than emotional impulse.

The *Bhagavad Gita* (2.54-2.57) describes the state of a **Sthitaprajna (one of steady wisdom)**:

"One who is unmoved by sorrow, who does not crave for pleasure, who is free from attachment, fear, and anger, is called a sage of steady wisdom."

3 Finding Inner Peace Amidst External Chaos

In a world filled with uncertainty, conflicts, and never-ending responsibilities, finding inner peace has become one of the most sought-after goals of modern life. The rapid pace of technology, societal pressures, and personal challenges often create an environment of stress, anxiety, and emotional turmoil. However, true peace is not dependent on external circumstances—it is an **inner state of being** that can be cultivated through self-awareness, resilience, and spiritual wisdom.

This essay explores the **importance of inner peace, the obstacles that prevent it, and practical steps to cultivate tranquility even amidst external chaos**. Drawing upon **philosophical teachings, psychological insights, and mindfulness practices**, we will understand how to navigate the turbulence of life without losing our sense of harmony.

Understanding Inner Peace

A. What is Inner Peace?

Inner peace is a **state of mental and emotional stability** where one remains unaffected by external disturbances. It is not the absence of challenges but the ability to remain calm, centered, and balanced regardless of life's circumstances.

- **Equanimity:** The ability to remain composed and unaffected by success or failure.

- **Mindfulness:** Being fully present and accepting life as it unfolds.

- **Detachment from negativity:** Not allowing external events to disturb one's inner state.

The *Bhagavad Gita* (2.15) teaches:

"The wise man who remains the same in pleasure and pain, whom these do not disturb, is fit for immortality."

This wisdom reminds us that true peace lies in our ability to detach from external chaos and find **stability within**.

B. The Modern Challenges to Inner Peace

In today's world, various factors contribute to inner unrest:

1. **Information Overload:** The constant bombardment of news, social media, and opinions creates mental clutter.

2. **Materialism and Comparison:** Society often equates success with material wealth, leading to stress and dissatisfaction.

3. **Emotional Turmoil:** Personal struggles, relationships, and work pressures can disturb mental balance.

4. **Uncertainty and Fear:** Economic instability, health concerns, and political unrest create anxiety.

Overcoming these challenges requires **a shift in perspective and conscious effort to cultivate inner tranquility**.

The Psychology of Inner Peace

A. How the Mind Reacts to Chaos

The human mind is wired to react to external threats through the **fight-or-flight response**, governed by the

amygdala. This reaction was useful in early human survival but is now triggered by modern stressors such as deadlines, criticism, or financial worries.

The **prefrontal cortex**, responsible for rational thinking and emotional regulation, can help override these automatic reactions. Practices like **mindfulness and meditation** strengthen this part of the brain, allowing individuals to respond to situations with clarity rather than impulsivity.

B. The Role of Emotional Regulation

People often lose inner peace due to unregulated emotions such as anger, fear, or resentment. **Cognitive Behavioral Therapy (CBT)** and **Self-Reflection Techniques** help individuals recognize and reframe negative thoughts, leading to emotional stability.

Spiritual and Philosophical Insights on Inner Peace

A. Stoicism: Accepting What We Cannot Control

The Stoic philosophers taught that inner peace comes from **focusing only on what is within our control** and accepting what is not.

- **Epictetus:** "Happiness and freedom begin with a clear understanding of one principle: Some things are within our control, and some things are not."

- **Marcus Aurelius:** "You have power over your mind—not outside events. Realize this, and you will find strength."

By shifting our focus inward, we free ourselves from unnecessary worry and distress.

B. Eastern Wisdom: The Middle Path

Buddhism emphasizes **the Middle Path**, which avoids extremes of indulgence and asceticism. By balancing material and spiritual pursuits, one attains **inner harmony**.

- **The Concept of Impermanence (Anicca):** Understanding that all experiences, both good and bad, are temporary helps us remain detached and at peace.

- **Mindfulness (Sati):** Being aware of the present moment prevents the mind from being consumed by regrets of the past or anxieties of the future.

Practical Strategies for Cultivating Inner Peace

A. Mindfulness and Meditation

Mindfulness helps anchor the mind in the **present moment**, preventing overthinking and anxiety. Practices include:

- **Breath Awareness:** Focusing on the breath to calm the mind.

- **Body Scan Meditation:** Observing bodily sensations to release tension.

- **Loving-Kindness Meditation:** Cultivating compassion towards oneself and others.

Scientific studies show that **regular meditation reduces stress, lowers blood pressure, and enhances emotional well-being**.

B. Detachment from External Outcomes

The *Bhagavad Gita* (2.47) teaches:

"You have the right to perform your duty, but never to the fruits of your work. Do not be attached to the results of your actions."

Practicing **Karma Yoga (selfless action without attachment to results)** allows individuals to work with dedication while remaining mentally free from worry and expectations.

C. Simplification and Minimalism

Excessive desires and material attachments often disturb inner peace. Minimalism encourages:

- **Decluttering physical and mental space.**

- **Focusing on experiences rather than possessions.**

- **Letting go of unnecessary commitments and toxic relationships.**

D. Gratitude and Acceptance

Cultivating gratitude shifts focus from what is lacking to what is already present. Daily practices include:

- **Gratitude journaling:** Writing three things one is grateful for each day.

- **Self-reflection:** Recognizing life's blessings rather than dwelling on problems.

Handling External Chaos with Inner Strength

A. Developing Emotional Resilience

Resilience is the ability to **bounce back from adversity**. Techniques to develop it include:

- **Reframing negative situations:** Seeing obstacles as opportunities for growth.

- **Practicing self-compassion:** Treating oneself with kindness during difficult times.

- **Seeking support:** Building strong relationships with supportive individuals.

B. Establishing Healthy Boundaries

To maintain inner peace, one must set **healthy boundaries** in personal and professional life:

- **Saying No:** Avoiding overcommitment to reduce stress.

- **Digital Detox:** Limiting social media consumption to prevent mental exhaustion.

- **Protecting Personal Space:** Ensuring time for rest, solitude, and self-care.

The Ultimate Freedom: Inner Peace as a Way of Life

Inner peace is **not a destination** but a lifelong practice. By making **mindfulness, detachment, resilience, and**

gratitude part of daily life, one can remain centered regardless of external circumstances.

The *Bhagavad Gita* (2.70) beautifully expresses this state:

"As the ocean remains unmoved by the waters entering it from all sides, so too the person who remains unmoved by desires attains peace."

This wisdom teaches that just as the ocean remains undisturbed by waves, a wise person remains unshaken by external events.

4 Psychological and Scientific Perspectives on Detachment and Equanimity

Detachment and equanimity are ancient philosophical concepts that have gained significant recognition in modern psychology and neuroscience. While detachment refers to the ability to remain emotionally independent from external circumstances, equanimity is the state of mental calmness and composure, especially in difficult situations. These qualities are essential for maintaining psychological well-being, reducing stress, and enhancing emotional intelligence.

This essay explores **the psychological and scientific foundations of detachment and equanimity, their benefits, and evidence-based practices** to cultivate these states of mind. We will examine how contemporary research in neuroscience, cognitive psychology, and behavioral therapy aligns with the wisdom of ancient traditions such as Stoicism and Buddhism.

Understanding Detachment and Equanimity

A. Defining Detachment and Equanimity

- **Detachment:** The ability to observe experiences without becoming emotionally overwhelmed or reactive. It does not mean indifference but rather an ability to maintain perspective and not be controlled by emotions.

- **Equanimity:** A state of psychological balance where one remains composed in both pleasurable and painful situations. It reflects an even-minded response to life's ups and downs.

In the *Bhagavad Gita* (2.50), it is stated:

"A wise person, unattached to success and failure, maintains equanimity and attains peace."

Similarly, Stoic philosopher Epictetus emphasized:

"It is not events that disturb us, but our perception of them."

These perspectives highlight the importance of detachment and equanimity in emotional well-being.

B. The Difference Between Healthy and Unhealthy Detachment

- **Healthy Detachment:** Involves emotional regulation, mindfulness, and acceptance. It allows individuals to engage fully in life without being consumed by stress or external validation.

- **Unhealthy Detachment:** Can manifest as emotional suppression, avoidance, or disinterest. This form of detachment may lead to social isolation and apathy.

Psychological research suggests that **balanced detachment enhances mental resilience**, while excessive emotional detachment may contribute to dissociation and alienation.

Psychological Foundations of Detachment and Equanimity

A. Cognitive Behavioral Therapy (CBT) and Emotional Regulation

CBT, a well-established psychological framework, helps individuals develop detachment and equanimity by altering their thought patterns. Core principles include:

1. **Cognitive Reframing:** Challenging irrational thoughts and replacing them with rational, balanced perspectives.

2. **Emotional Regulation:** Techniques such as deep breathing and mindfulness to prevent emotional overwhelm.

3. **Exposure Therapy:** Encouraging gradual exposure to stressors to build resilience and reduce reactivity.

CBT aligns with the **Stoic practice of premeditatio malorum** (anticipating adversity), which trains the mind to accept challenges without fear or distress.

B. The Role of Mindfulness and Meditation

Mindfulness practices cultivate detachment and equanimity by training the brain to observe thoughts without identification. **Neuroscientific studies show that regular meditation enhances**:

- **Prefrontal Cortex Functioning:** Responsible for rational thinking and emotional control.

- **Amygdala Regulation:** Reducing fear-based responses and emotional impulsivity.

- **Neuroplasticity:** Strengthening neural pathways associated with self-awareness and resilience.

A study published in *Psychosomatic Medicine* (Davidson et al., 2003) found that **long-term meditators exhibited greater emotional stability and lower stress levels**, supporting the psychological benefits of equanimity.

C. Emotional Intelligence and Self-Detachment

Daniel Goleman's theory of **Emotional Intelligence (EI)** suggests that self-awareness and self-regulation are critical to achieving equanimity. Components include:

- **Self-Awareness:** Recognizing and understanding one's emotions.

- **Self-Regulation:** Managing emotional responses effectively.

- **Empathy:** Understanding others without emotional over-identification.

Studies show that individuals with higher EI are better equipped to **handle stress, maintain balanced relationships, and exhibit psychological resilience**.

Neuroscientific Insights into Equanimity and Detachment

A. The Brain's Response to Stress and Equanimity

Equanimity involves a well-balanced interaction between different brain regions:

- **Amygdala:** The emotional center of the brain, responsible for fear and stress responses. Equanimity reduces its hyperactivity.

- **Prefrontal Cortex:** Regulates decision-making and emotional control, strengthened through mindfulness and meditation.

- **Default Mode Network (DMN):** A network involved in mind-wandering and self-referential thoughts. Equanimity practices reduce DMN activity, leading to decreased overthinking and anxiety.

Functional MRI (fMRI) studies indicate that **Buddhist monks and advanced meditators exhibit lower amygdala activation and greater prefrontal cortex engagement**, signifying improved emotional control.

B. Neurochemical Changes Associated with Equanimity

1. **Reduced Cortisol Levels:** Cortisol is the stress hormone responsible for anxiety. Meditation and

detachment practices have been shown to lower cortisol levels, promoting relaxation.

2. **Increased Serotonin and Dopamine:** These neurotransmitters regulate mood and contribute to a sense of well-being and contentment.

3. **Higher Oxytocin Release:** Supports emotional bonding and social connection without excessive attachment.

Scientific evidence supports the claim that **cultivating equanimity through mindfulness can create lasting neurological changes** that enhance emotional resilience.

Practical Techniques to Cultivate Detachment and Equanimity

A. Mindfulness-Based Stress Reduction (MBSR)

Developed by Jon Kabat-Zinn, MBSR incorporates meditation, breath awareness, and body scanning to enhance emotional regulation. Clinical studies show that **MBSR significantly reduces anxiety, depression, and emotional reactivity**.

B. Stoic Practices for Detachment

- **Negative Visualization:** Imagining worst-case scenarios to reduce fear and increase gratitude.

- **Voluntary Discomfort:** Engaging in small discomforts (e.g., fasting, cold showers) to build emotional resilience.

- **Dichotomy of Control:** Accepting that some things are within our control, while others are not.

C. Cognitive Distancing

Cognitive distancing is a psychological technique used to **observe one's thoughts from a third-person perspective**. Strategies include:

- **Journaling:** Writing thoughts down to gain perspective.

- **Talking to Oneself in the Third Person:** Research suggests that self-talk in the third person reduces emotional intensity.

D. Gratitude and Perspective Shifting

- **Daily Gratitude Practice:** Shifting focus from what is lacking to what is present.

- **Practicing Radical Acceptance:** Acknowledging reality without resistance.

The Psychological and Social Benefits of Equanimity

A. Enhanced Mental Health

Studies indicate that individuals who cultivate equanimity experience:

- **Lower anxiety and depression levels.**

- **Improved emotional stability.**

- **Reduced symptoms of PTSD and chronic stress.**

B. Stronger Relationships

Equanimity fosters **compassion, patience, and non-reactivity**, leading to healthier relationships. By reducing emotional over-identification, individuals can engage with others without losing their sense of self.

C. Improved Decision-Making

Detachment from emotional impulses allows for:

- **Rational and objective thinking.**

- **Reduced susceptibility to cognitive biases.**

- **Better conflict resolution and leadership skills.**

5 The Art of Living with Detachment and Equanimity

Life is an unpredictable journey filled with both joy and suffering. The ability to navigate through life's fluctuations with stability and peace is an art that requires deep understanding and practice. **Detachment and equanimity** are two essential qualities that allow individuals to remain balanced amidst the inevitable ups and downs of life. These concepts have been extensively explored in ancient spiritual traditions such as Buddhism, Stoicism, and Hinduism, and they have gained recognition in modern psychology and neuroscience.

Detachment does not imply indifference but rather a mindful disengagement from unhealthy attachments, while equanimity refers to maintaining mental composure in both favorable and unfavorable circumstances. Together, they form a foundation for living with clarity, resilience, and inner peace.

This essay explores **the philosophy, psychology, and scientific understanding of detachment and equanimity**, along with practical methods to cultivate these virtues for a more fulfilling life.

The Meaning and Philosophy of Detachment and Equanimity

A. Understanding Detachment

- **Definition:** Detachment is the ability to remain emotionally independent from external circumstances while maintaining engagement in life.

- **Types of Detachment:**

  - *Healthy Detachment:* Conscious and mindful distancing from emotional reactivity.

  - *Unhealthy Detachment:* Emotional suppression, avoidance, or disinterest.

Ancient wisdom traditions emphasize that true detachment is about engaging fully in life while maintaining a sense of **inner freedom**. The *Bhagavad Gita* (2.47) states:

> *"You have the right to perform your duty, but never to the fruits of your actions."*

This principle teaches that one should act without excessive attachment to outcomes, leading to mental peace and fulfillment.

B. Understanding Equanimity

- **Definition:** Equanimity is the ability to maintain a calm and balanced state of mind, regardless of external conditions.

- **Equanimity in Stoicism and Buddhism:**

  - Stoics practiced *apatheia*, which refers to freedom from destructive emotions.

  - Buddhism teaches *upekkha*, a form of deep inner peace and acceptance.

Epictetus, a Stoic philosopher, stated:

"It's not what happens to you, but how you react to it that matters."

Thus, equanimity is not about suppressing emotions but about **responding with wisdom rather than reactivity**.

Psychological and Scientific Perspectives on Detachment and Equanimity

A. Psychological Theories on Emotional Regulation

- **Cognitive Behavioral Therapy (CBT):**

  - Teaches cognitive reframing to manage emotional responses.

  - Encourages mindfulness and non-reactivity.

- **Emotional Intelligence (EI):**

  - Self-awareness and self-regulation enhance equanimity.

- o Empathy and detachment prevent emotional exhaustion.

B. Neuroscience of Detachment and Equanimity

Scientific studies suggest that **equanimity and detachment lead to neurological changes that enhance resilience**:

- **Reduced Amygdala Activity:** The amygdala, which regulates fear and emotions, becomes less reactive with mindfulness and meditation.

- **Enhanced Prefrontal Cortex Functioning:** The prefrontal cortex, responsible for rational thinking and decision-making, becomes more active.

- **Lower Cortisol Levels:** Detachment and equanimity practices reduce stress hormones, improving overall well-being.

Studies on Buddhist monks have shown that long-term meditation **reduces emotional volatility and increases happiness**, providing scientific validation for these ancient practices.

Practical Techniques to Cultivate Detachment and Equanimity

A. Mindfulness and Meditation Practices

Mindfulness practices help in observing thoughts and emotions without attachment. Techniques include:

- **Breath Awareness Meditation:** Focusing on the breath to stay present.

- **Loving-Kindness Meditation:** Cultivating compassion while maintaining emotional boundaries.

- **Body Scan Meditation:** Developing awareness of bodily sensations without reacting emotionally.

B. Stoic Practices for Equanimity

1. **Negative Visualization:** Imagining worst-case scenarios to reduce fear and increase gratitude.

2. **Voluntary Discomfort:** Practicing small discomforts (e.g., fasting, cold showers) to build emotional resilience.

3. **Dichotomy of Control:** Accepting what is within our control and letting go of what is not.

C. Journaling and Self-Reflection

- **Gratitude Journaling:** Shifting focus from what is lacking to what is present.

- **Cognitive Distancing:** Writing thoughts in the third person to gain perspective.

- **Daily Reflection:** Analyzing daily experiences to cultivate awareness and non-attachment.

D. Practicing Detachment in Relationships and Work

1. **Detachment in Relationships:** Loving and caring without excessive emotional dependence.

2. **Detachment at Work:** Performing duties with dedication while maintaining emotional balance.

3. **Detachment from Social Media:** Reducing exposure to negativity and external validation.

The Benefits of Living with Detachment and Equanimity

A. Enhanced Mental and Emotional Health

- **Reduced Anxiety and Depression:** Emotional stability reduces the likelihood of mental health disorders.

- **Greater Emotional Resilience:** Ability to handle life's uncertainties with composure.

- **Lower Stress Levels:** Mindful detachment reduces stress-related illnesses.

B. Improved Relationships

- **Healthier Boundaries:** Detachment prevents emotional exhaustion and codependency.

- **Greater Empathy:** Understanding others without absorbing their emotions.

- **Less Conflict:** Non-reactivity reduces impulsive arguments and misunderstandings.

C. Increased Productivity and Focus

- **Better Decision-Making:** Detachment from immediate emotions leads to rational choices.

- **Higher Concentration:** Equanimity reduces distractions and enhances work efficiency.

- **Greater Creativity:** A calm mind fosters innovative thinking.

Overcoming Challenges in Practicing Detachment and Equanimity

A. Dealing with Emotional Attachments

- **Mindful Observation:** Acknowledge emotions without identifying with them.

- **Gradual Practice:** Start with small steps, such as detaching from minor frustrations.

- **Seeking Guidance:** Learn from mentors, therapists, or spiritual teachers.

B. Addressing Fear of Indifference

- **Understanding True Detachment:** It is not about emotional suppression but about balanced engagement.

- **Practicing Compassion with Boundaries:** Love and care without excessive identification.

- **Regular Reflection:** Assessing personal growth to ensure a healthy balance.

C. Handling Social Pressures

- **Building Inner Confidence:** Relying on internal validation rather than external approval.

- **Selective Engagement:** Choosing meaningful interactions over superficial ones.

- **Developing Self-Compassion:** Accepting oneself despite societal expectations.

Conclusion

Detachment and equanimity are not mere philosophical ideals but practical tools for achieving lasting peace and resilience. A **Sthitaprajna** embodies these qualities, living with awareness, balance, and wisdom. By cultivating a **detached yet engaged** approach to life, one can experience true freedom—free from the turmoil of attachment and the instability of emotions.

As Lord Krishna teaches, the highest art of living is **to act wholeheartedly yet remain unattached to the fruits of action**. In mastering this art, we unlock the potential to live with clarity, joy, and an unshakable inner peace.

Chapter 06: The Role of Devotion: Bhakti as Supreme Love

The significance of surrender to the Divine

Love and faith in Krishna's teachings

Universal devotion beyond religious boundaries

Introduction

Devotion, or **Bhakti**, is often described as the highest form of love—pure, selfless, and unconditional. Unlike worldly love, which is often tainted by desire and expectations, Bhakti is centered on complete surrender to the Divine. It is a spiritual path that transcends religious boundaries, leading one to a profound connection with the Supreme Being. This essay explores the significance of surrender, the essence of love and faith in Krishna's teachings, and the universal nature of devotion.

1 The Significance of Surrender to the Divine

Surrender to the Divine is one of the most profound spiritual concepts found across various religious and philosophical traditions. It signifies the complete offering of oneself—body, mind, and soul—to the Supreme Power, acknowledging that divine will supersedes personal desires. True surrender is not about resignation or passivity but about **trust, faith, and the realization that the Divine knows what is best for us**. This essay delves deeply into the significance of surrender, its role in different spiritual traditions, its transformative power, and its impact on personal and collective well-being.

Understanding Surrender: A Spiritual Perspective

Surrender (*Sharanagati* in Sanskrit) is often misunderstood as giving up one's free will or personal strength. However, in a spiritual sense, it means relinquishing ego-driven desires and aligning oneself with divine consciousness. It is the recognition that human intellect, no matter how advanced, has limitations and that true wisdom comes from **yielding to the higher power**.

Defining Surrender

Surrender involves:

- **Letting go of control:** Understanding that we do not have complete control over life's outcomes.

- **Trusting divine guidance:** Believing that the Divine will always lead us to what is best for our soul's growth.

- **Detachment from ego:** Releasing the need for personal gain and recognizing that everything happens according to a divine plan.

Krishna's Call to Surrender

In the *Bhagavad Gita*, Lord Krishna states:

Sarva-dharmān parityajya mām ekaṁ śaraṇaṁ vraja (Abandon all varieties of duties and just surrender unto Me. I shall deliver you from all sinful reactions. Do not fear.) (BG 18.66)

This verse encapsulates the essence of surrender—letting go of all doubts, anxieties, and attachments, and entrusting oneself completely to the Divine.

The Role of Surrender in Different Spiritual Traditions

Surrender is a common theme across various religious and spiritual traditions. While the expressions may differ, the underlying principle remains the same: **trust in the Divine leads to liberation, peace, and fulfillment**.

Hinduism: Bhakti and Surrender

In Hinduism, Bhakti (*devotion*) is considered the highest form of surrender. Saints like Mirabai, Tulsidas, and Ramanuja emphasized that true devotion arises when a devotee ceases to see themselves as separate from the Divine.

- **Mirabai's Devotion to Krishna:** She abandoned societal expectations and surrendered herself completely to Krishna, finding solace and divine love.

- **The Ramanuja Tradition:** This school of thought teaches *prapatti* (absolute surrender), where the devotee places complete faith in Lord Vishnu, trusting Him for ultimate liberation.

Islam: Submission to the Will of Allah

The word *Islam* itself means **submission**. Surrendering to Allah's will is the foundation of Islamic faith.

- **Tawakkul (Trust in Allah):** Believers are encouraged to place their trust in God and accept His plans.

- **Sufi Mysticism:** Sufi saints like Rumi and Hafiz wrote extensively about surrendering the ego to experience divine love.

Christianity: The Power of Faith and Submission

Christianity teaches that faith in God requires surrendering personal will and trusting in divine guidance.

- **Jesus' Surrender:** In the Garden of Gethsemane, Jesus prayed, "Not my will, but Thine be done" (Luke 22:42), demonstrating complete submission to God's plan.

- **Saints and Mystics:** St. Francis of Assisi and Mother Teresa exemplified surrender through service, faith, and devotion.

Buddhism: Letting Go of Attachment

While Buddhism does not focus on a personal God, it teaches **surrendering attachment** to desires and ego as a path to enlightenment.

- **The Middle Path:** The Buddha taught that suffering arises from attachment, and surrendering desires leads to liberation (*Nirvana*).

- **Zen Teachings:** Zen Buddhism emphasizes surrendering to the present moment and embracing reality as it is.

The Transformative Power of Surrender

Surrendering to the Divine leads to **profound inner transformation**. It brings peace, resilience, and a deeper connection to life's purpose.

Freedom from Fear and Anxiety

- **Letting Go of Worry:** When we surrender to the Divine, we no longer carry the burden of controlling everything.

- **Trusting the Process:** Knowing that everything happens for a reason brings peace and acceptance.

Enhancing Spiritual Growth

- **Deepening Faith:** The more we surrender, the more our faith grows.

- **Opening to Divine Guidance:** Surrender creates space for intuition and divine wisdom to flow.

Living in the Present Moment

- **Detachment from Outcomes:** When we surrender, we focus on actions without obsessing over results.

- **Acceptance and Gratitude:** A surrendered life is one of gratitude, as everything is seen as divine grace.

The Challenges of Surrender

Surrender is not always easy. It requires patience, trust, and perseverance.

Overcoming Ego and Pride

- **Ego Resists Surrender:** The human mind wants control and resists letting go.

- **Practices to Overcome Ego:** Meditation, prayer, and humility help in dissolving ego.

Handling Uncertainty

- **Fear of the Unknown:** Many struggle to surrender because they fear uncertainty.

- **Building Trust in the Divine:** Reflecting on past experiences where surrender led to positive outcomes can strengthen faith.

Practices to Cultivate Surrender

Surrender is a continuous process that can be cultivated through spiritual discipline and inner reflection.

Prayer and Devotion

- **Daily Prayer:** Talking to the Divine helps reinforce trust and surrender.

- **Chanting and Mantras:** Repeating sacred names or verses helps in calming the mind and deepening faith.

Meditation and Mindfulness

- **Silent Meditation:** Helps in observing thoughts and detaching from ego.

- **Mindfulness Practices:** Being present in every moment reduces resistance to divine flow.

Acts of Service and Selflessness

- **Karma Yoga:** Performing selfless service without expecting rewards fosters surrender.

- **Helping Others:** Serving others with love and devotion strengthens faith in the divine order.

The Ultimate Reward: Divine Grace and Liberation

Surrender is the key to receiving **divine grace**. When we let go, we open ourselves to the boundless blessings of the universe.

Miracles of Surrender

- **Draupadi's Unwavering Faith:** When Draupadi was humiliated, she surrendered completely to Krishna, and divine intervention saved her.

- **Prahlada's Devotion:** Despite torture from his father, Prahlada's faith in Vishnu led to divine protection.

Liberation from the Cycle of Birth and Death

- **Moksha in Hinduism:** Surrender leads to liberation from material existence.

- **Salvation in Christianity and Islam:** True surrender brings eternal peace and union with the Divine.

2 Love and Faith in Krishna's Teachings

Krishna's teachings emphasize love (*prema*) and faith (*shraddha*) as the foundation of Bhakti. His message in the *Bhagavad Gita* and other sacred texts highlights the importance of devotion as the simplest yet most profound path to divine realization.

Bhakti: The Path of Love

In the *Bhakti Yoga* tradition, love is not just an emotion but a spiritual force that binds the devotee to the Divine. Krishna exemplifies this through His **Rasa Lila** with the Gopis, symbolizing the soul's longing for union with God.

- **Selfless Love:** The devotion of Radha for Krishna is often considered the epitome of pure, selfless love. Radha's love was not based on material gains or personal desires; it was an **eternal longing** to merge with Krishna.

- **Devotion Over Rituals:** Krishna teaches that God does not seek grand offerings or complex rituals but rather the **sincerity of the heart**. In the *Bhagavad Gita*, He says:

Patram puṣpam phalam toyam yo me bhaktyā prayacchati
(Whoever offers Me a leaf, a flower, a fruit, or water with love, I accept it.) (BG 9.26)

This verse emphasizes that God values **love and faith over material wealth**.

Faith as the Cornerstone of Devotion

Faith (*shraddha*) is an essential aspect of Bhakti. Without faith, devotion remains superficial and cannot withstand challenges.

- **The Example of Draupadi:** When Draupadi was humiliated in the Kaurava court, she initially sought help from her husbands and elders. But when all failed, she completely surrendered to Krishna with unwavering faith. Her faith invoked divine intervention, and Krishna saved her, demonstrating that **true faith never goes unanswered**.

- **Prahlada's Unshakable Devotion:** The story of Prahlada, a young devotee of Vishnu, is another example of unwavering faith. Despite being tormented by his father, King Hiranyakashipu, Prahlada's faith in Lord Vishnu remained strong. His devotion ultimately led to Vishnu's manifestation as Narasimha to protect him, proving that **faith in the Divine overcomes even the greatest adversities**.

Universal Devotion Beyond Religious Boundaries

In a world divided by religious, cultural, and ideological differences, the concept of **universal devotion** serves as a bridge that unites humanity beyond sectarian beliefs. Devotion is often associated with a particular faith, deity, or religious tradition, but at its core, it transcends all boundaries, embodying **universal love, faith, and surrender to a higher power or higher purpose**. True devotion is not limited to rituals or doctrines but manifests as **pure love, compassion, and selflessness**, uniting all beings in a shared spiritual experience.

This essay explores the essence of universal devotion, how it transcends religious barriers, its significance in fostering global harmony, and its expression through different spiritual traditions and philosophies.

Understanding Universal Devotion

Defining Devotion Beyond Religion

Devotion (*bhakti* in Sanskrit) is often misunderstood as adherence to a particular religious path. However, **true devotion is not about belonging to a specific faith but about an inner connection to the divine, humanity, and the universe**. Universal devotion is characterized by:

- **Unconditional Love** – Love that is beyond expectations, judgments, and personal gain.

- **Faith and Trust** – Believing in a higher purpose without the need for rigid dogmas.

- **Compassion for All** – Seeing the divine in every being and serving them selflessly.

- **Surrender and Humility** – Letting go of ego and personal desires in service to a higher power.

Universal devotion is the **recognition that divinity exists beyond religious constructs**, making it accessible to all, regardless of religious identity.

Love as the Core of Devotion

Saints, mystics, and philosophers across traditions have emphasized that **love is the highest form of devotion**. This love is not confined to religious institutions but extends to all of creation. **Love in devotion is pure,**

unconditional, and selfless, reflecting the unity of all beings.

As Rumi, the Sufi poet, beautifully expressed:

"The religion of love is separate from all religions: For lovers, the only religion and faith is God."

This statement encapsulates the essence of universal devotion—one that surpasses religious identities and unites all through divine love.

Universal Devotion in Different Spiritual Traditions

Though religions may differ in beliefs, their core essence of devotion remains the same. Various traditions emphasize **love, service, and surrender**, proving that devotion transcends religious boundaries.

Hinduism: Bhakti as a Universal Force

The **Bhakti movement** in Hinduism emphasized **love and devotion as the simplest means of attaining the divine**. Saints like Mirabai, Tulsidas, and Kabir preached that **true devotion is about love, not rituals**.

- **Mirabai's Devotion to Krishna:** Despite social restrictions, Mirabai devoted herself to Krishna, showcasing devotion beyond religious orthodoxy.

- **Kabir's Teachings:** Kabir, born into a weaver's family, criticized religious dogma and emphasized **oneness with the Divine, beyond Hindu-Muslim divisions**.

Islam: Sufi Mysticism and Love for the Divine

Sufism, the mystical branch of Islam, focuses on **love, unity, and surrender** rather than religious laws.

- **Rumi's Universal Devotion:** His poetry expresses **oneness with God and love beyond religious labels**.

- **Rabia al-Adawiyya's Divine Love:** She declared, *"O God! If I worship You for fear of hell, burn me in hell. If I worship You for hope of paradise, deny me paradise. But if I worship You for Your own sake, do not withhold Your Everlasting Beauty from me."* This shows devotion beyond personal gain.

Christianity: Love and Devotion to Humanity

Christianity teaches that devotion to God is expressed through **love for others**.

- **Jesus' Message of Universal Love:** Jesus emphasized that love for God and love for humanity are inseparable.

- **Saint Francis of Assisi:** He served the poor and saw divine presence in all beings, embodying **universal devotion beyond church boundaries**.

Buddhism: Compassion as Devotion

Buddhism does not focus on a personal God but emphasizes **devotion through compassion and selflessness**.

- **Bodhisattva Ideal:** In Mahayana Buddhism, Bodhisattvas dedicate themselves to the enlightenment of all beings, showing **devotion beyond personal salvation**.

- **Dalai Lama's Teachings:** He promotes **compassion and kindness as the highest forms of devotion**.

Sikhism: Devotion through Service

Guru Nanak, the founder of Sikhism, taught that devotion is not about rituals but about **service to humanity**.

- **Langar (Community Kitchen):** Providing free food to all, regardless of religion, demonstrates **universal devotion in action**.

- **Ek Onkar (One God):** Sikhism preaches that there is **only one divine force, beyond religious labels**.

These examples show that while religions may differ in form, their essence of **devotion as love, service, and surrender remains universal**.

The Impact of Universal Devotion on Society

Beyond individual spiritual growth, universal devotion has a profound impact on society. It fosters **unity, peace, and compassion** among diverse groups.

Fostering Unity and Tolerance

- **Devotion unites, dogma divides:** Religious institutions often create divisions, but devotion emphasizes the **oneness of humanity**.

- **Interfaith Harmony:** When devotion is seen as universal, it becomes a force for **bridging gaps between religions**.

Overcoming Religious Conflicts

- **True devotion is not about superiority:** Many religious conflicts arise from claims of superiority, but **universal devotion teaches that all paths lead to the Divine**.

- **Respecting Differences:** When people embrace devotion beyond boundaries, they respect other faiths without feeling threatened.

Encouraging Selfless Service

- **Devotion is expressed through action:** Serving others selflessly is a true mark of devotion, as seen in organizations like the Red Cross, Ramakrishna Mission, and Sufi charity work.

- **Eliminating Discrimination:** Universal devotion sees all as equal, challenging caste, race, and gender discrimination.

Challenges to Universal Devotion

While universal devotion is a powerful concept, several obstacles prevent its widespread acceptance.

Religious Exclusivism

- Many religious institutions claim that **their path is the only true path**, discouraging devotion beyond their faith.

- Overcoming this requires **education and interfaith dialogue**.

Ego and Sectarian Identity

- People often associate devotion with their religious identity, making it difficult to accept **devotion beyond their belief system**.

- Spiritual leaders must **emphasize commonalities rather than differences**.

Materialism and Lack of Faith

- Modern society prioritizes **material success over spiritual devotion**, making universal devotion seem impractical.

- The solution lies in **reviving spiritual values through education and practice**.

Practicing Universal Devotion in Daily Life

Embracing universal devotion requires conscious effort. Here are practical ways to cultivate it:

Love and Compassion for All

- Treat every being with **kindness, respect, and empathy**.

- Avoid discrimination based on religion, caste, or nationality.

Engaging in Selfless Service

- Participate in **charity, community service, and humanitarian efforts**.

- Help those in need without expecting rewards.

Respecting All Faiths

- Learn about other religions with **an open heart and mind**.

- Participate in **interfaith discussions and events**.

Meditation and Inner Reflection

- Develop personal **devotion through meditation, prayer, or mindfulness**.

- Focus on the **essence of love and surrender rather than external rituals**.

3 The Transformative Power of Bhakti

Bhakti, or devotion, is one of the most profound and transformative forces in human life. Rooted in the Sanskrit word *bhaj*, meaning "to share" or "to belong," Bhakti represents an **intense love and devotion to the Divine**. While often associated with Hindu traditions, Bhakti transcends religious boundaries and is found in various spiritual traditions across the world. It is a path that fosters **inner transformation, self-realization, and a deep connection with the Divine**.

The transformative power of Bhakti lies in its ability to **elevate the soul, purify the heart, and dissolve the ego**, leading to a state of divine love and surrender. This essay explores the profound impact of Bhakti, its role in different traditions, its psychological and emotional benefits, and its power to bring social and personal transformation.

Understanding Bhakti: A Path of Divine Love

Bhakti is often described as **the highest form of love**, an unconditional and selfless devotion to the Divine. It is **not limited to religious rituals but is an internal, deeply personal experience**. Bhakti can manifest in various forms, such as **prayer, music, dance, poetry, service, and meditation**.

The Essence of Bhakti

- **Unconditional Love**: True Bhakti is devoid of expectations and seeks nothing in return.

- **Surrender (Sharanagati)**: The devotee completely surrenders to the Divine, accepting its will with total faith.

- **Constant Remembrance (Smaran)**: The devotee keeps the Divine in their thoughts at all times, cultivating an intimate connection.

- **Selflessness (Nishkama Bhakti)**: Devotion without selfish motives, focusing solely on loving the Divine.

- **Emotional Purity**: Bhakti cleanses negative emotions such as ego, pride, and material attachments.

The Different Forms of Bhakti

Bhakti is expressed in various ways, depending on the temperament and inclination of the devotee. In Hindu philosophy, the **Navadha Bhakti (Nine Forms of Devotion)** describes different ways of expressing Bhakti:

1. **Shravana (Listening)** – Hearing stories and teachings of the Divine.

2. **Kirtana (Chanting)** – Singing or reciting the Divine's name.

3. **Smarana (Remembering)** – Keeping the Divine in one's thoughts constantly.

4. **Padasevana (Serving the Divine's Feet)** – Serving others as a form of worship.

5. **Archana (Worship)** – Performing rituals and offerings with love.

6. **Vandana (Prayer and Prostration)** – Humbling oneself before the Divine.

7. **Dasya (Servitude)** – Seeing oneself as a servant of the Divine.

8. **Sakhya (Friendship)** – Establishing an intimate, friendly bond with the Divine.

9. **Atmanivedana (Surrender)** – Giving oneself completely to the Divine.

These forms show that Bhakti is not rigid but **highly personal and adaptable**, allowing each individual to connect with the Divine in their own way.

Bhakti in Different Spiritual Traditions

Although Bhakti is deeply rooted in Hinduism, similar forms of devotion exist in other religions, proving that **the path of divine love is universal.**

Hinduism: The Bhakti Movement

The Bhakti movement in medieval India was a spiritual revolution that emphasized **love over rituals, devotion over dogma, and surrender over intellectualism**. Saints like Mirabai, Tulsidas, Surdas, and Kabir rejected social barriers and emphasized **a direct, personal relationship with the Divine**.

- **Mirabai's Love for Krishna:** Mirabai's songs express an unconditional and passionate love for Krishna, symbolizing Bhakti's transformative power.

- **Kabir's Philosophy:** Kabir, a poet-saint, emphasized devotion beyond religious distinctions, saying, *"God is neither Hindu nor Muslim; He dwells in the heart of the devotee."*

Christianity: Love for God and Humanity

Christianity, particularly through figures like **Saint Francis of Assisi, Mother Teresa, and mystics like Saint John of the Cross**, emphasizes love and devotion to God through service to humanity.

- **Jesus' Teaching of Love:** *"Love the Lord your God with all your heart, soul, and mind, and love your neighbor as yourself."*

- **Christian Mysticism:** The works of Saint Teresa of Avila and Saint Augustine reflect Bhakti-like devotion in the Christian tradition.

Islam: Sufi Devotion and Divine Love

Sufism, the mystical path of Islam, mirrors Bhakti in its **intense longing for union with the Divine**.

- **Rumi's Poetry:** *"Lose yourself completely, return to the root of the root of your own soul."*

- **Rabia al-Adawiyya's Love for God:** She loved God so intensely that she rejected worship based on fear of hell or hope for paradise, focusing only on divine love.

Buddhism: Devotion through Compassion

- **Bodhisattva Ideal:** In Mahayana Buddhism, Bodhisattvas dedicate themselves to the welfare of all beings, reflecting Bhakti's selfless love.

- **Pure Land Buddhism:** Devotion to Amitabha Buddha, reciting his name with love and surrender, mirrors Bhakti traditions.

The Psychological and Emotional Transformation through Bhakti

Bhakti is not only a spiritual path but also a **therapeutic force** that transforms the mind and heart.

Purification of the Heart

- Removes **anger, ego, greed, and jealousy**.

- Replaces negativity with **love, patience, and humility**.

Mental Peace and Stability

- Devotion reduces **anxiety, stress, and depression**.

- Cultivating surrender leads to **freedom from worry and fear**.

Strengthening Emotional Resilience

- Devotees develop **unshakable faith in divine protection**.

- Surrendering to the Divine helps navigate life's challenges with grace.

The Social Impact of Bhakti

Bhakti is not just personal; it has transformed societies by breaking barriers and inspiring selfless service.

Equality and Social Reform

- Saints like **Kabir and Guru Nanak** opposed caste discrimination and preached equality.

- Bhakti movements have **challenged gender biases** by promoting female saints and leaders.

Service to Humanity

- Organizations like **ISKCON, Ramakrishna Mission, and Sufi charities** promote selfless service through Bhakti.

- **Langar in Sikhism** (community kitchens) embody the spirit of Bhakti by feeding all, regardless of religion or status.

Practicing Bhakti in Daily Life

Bhakti is not limited to temples or rituals—it can be integrated into everyday life through:

1. **Chanting and Prayers** – Regular recitation of divine names brings mental peace.

2. **Acts of Compassion** – Serving others selflessly is an expression of devotion.

3. **Meditation on the Divine** – Visualizing the Divine strengthens connection.

4. **Gratitude and Surrender** – Accepting life with faith and gratitude enhances Bhakti.

5. **Seeing the Divine in All** – Treating every being with love and respect is the highest form of devotion.

Conclusion

Bhakti, as the supreme form of love, teaches us that true devotion is not about rituals, offerings, or religious affiliations, but about **surrender, faith, and universal love**. Krishna's teachings emphasize that **anyone, regardless of background, can attain divine grace through love and devotion**. Bhakti transcends all boundaries and unites humanity in the pursuit of spiritual fulfillment.

In a world divided by differences, the path of Bhakti serves as a reminder that love for the Divine is the greatest unifier, leading us beyond material existence into eternal bliss. Through surrender, faith, and selfless love, one can truly experience **Bhakti as Supreme Love**.

Chapter 07: Karma and Reincarnation: The Cycle of Action and Consequence

Introduction

The concepts of karma and reincarnation have been central to many philosophical and religious traditions, particularly in Hinduism, Buddhism, and Jainism. These ideas provide a framework for understanding the consequences of human actions and the cycle of life, death, and rebirth. The principle of karma asserts that every action—good or bad—produces corresponding results, shaping an individual's present and future experiences. Reincarnation, on the other hand, refers to the belief that the soul is reborn into new life forms based on past karmic deeds. Together, these doctrines offer a profound explanation of human existence, moral responsibility, and the pursuit of liberation (moksha).

1 The Law of Cause and Effect

The concept of cause and effect is a fundamental principle that governs the universe. It asserts that every action has a consequence, whether immediate or delayed. This principle is observed in natural sciences, philosophy, psychology, and spiritual traditions, providing a framework for understanding the interconnectedness of events. In Eastern philosophies, particularly in Hinduism, Buddhism, and Jainism, this idea manifests as the law of karma, where every deed influences future experiences. In Western thought, it aligns with Newton's Third Law— "For every action, there is an equal and opposite reaction." This discussion explores the law of cause and effect from various perspectives, including scientific, philosophical, ethical, and spiritual dimensions.

At its core, karma is the law of cause and effect, suggesting that every action has a corresponding reaction. It is often summarized as "what goes around comes around." This principle applies not only to individual actions but also to thoughts and intentions. In Hindu philosophy, karma is classified into three types:

1. **Sanchita Karma**: The accumulated karma from past lives that influence the present life.

2. **Prarabdha Karma**: The portion of sanchita karma that is currently being experienced in this life.

3. **Kriyamana Karma**: The karma generated by present actions, which will affect the future.

This law implies that individuals are responsible for their own fate, as their past and present actions determine their future circumstances. Unlike a deterministic outlook, karma provides a dynamic approach to life, suggesting that one can shape their destiny through righteous actions.

Scientific Perspectives on Cause and Effect

In science, the law of cause and effect is foundational. Every event or phenomenon has a preceding cause, which can be studied and analyzed through observation and experimentation.

1. **Physics and the Law of Causality**

- o Classical physics, based on Newtonian mechanics, operates on deterministic causality, meaning that given a set of initial conditions, outcomes can be predicted.

- o In thermodynamics, cause and effect are evident in energy transfer processes. For example, heat applied to an object causes it to expand.

- o Quantum mechanics challenges strict determinism by introducing probabilities, yet even in quantum physics, cause-effect relationships exist at statistical levels.

2. **Biology and Evolution**

- o In biological systems, cause and effect can be seen in genetics and evolution. Genetic mutations cause variations in species, leading to evolutionary changes over generations.

- o In ecology, environmental factors influence the survival and behavior of organisms, showing clear cause-effect relationships.

3. **Psychology and Behavioral Sciences**

- o Human behavior is often a result of cause-and-effect interactions, including conditioning, cognitive processing, and emotional responses.

- o Studies in neuroscience indicate that brain activity causes specific thoughts and behaviors, further reinforcing the principle.

Philosophical and Ethical Interpretations

Philosophers have long debated the nature of causality and its implications for free will, determinism, and moral responsibility.

1. **Determinism vs. Free Will**

   - o Determinism suggests that every event is predetermined by prior causes, leaving no room for free will.

   - o Compatibilists argue that free will and causality can coexist, where human choices arise from prior influences but still allow moral responsibility.

2. **Ethical Considerations**

   - o Cause and effect play a role in moral decision-making. Good actions lead to positive outcomes, while negative actions result in adverse consequences.

   - o Injustice and suffering are often examined through this lens, questioning whether past causes justify present experiences.

Spiritual and Religious Perspectives

1. **Hinduism and Karma**

o The law of karma states that every action (physical, mental, or verbal) has a consequence, affecting future reincarnations and life circumstances.

o Hindu scriptures, like the Bhagavad Gita, emphasize performing righteous actions without attachment to results (Nishkama Karma).

2. **Buddhism and Cause-Effect in Suffering**

o The Four Noble Truths explain that suffering (dukkha) arises due to causes such as attachment and ignorance. By eliminating these causes, suffering ceases.

o The concept of dependent origination (pratītyasamutpāda) explains how all phenomena arise from interdependent causes.

3. **Christianity and Divine Justice**

o Christianity acknowledges cause and effect through the principle of divine justice—good deeds lead to blessings, while sins result in consequences.

o The Bible's teachings reinforce the idea that "as you sow, so shall you reap."

Modern-Day Applications of Cause and Effect

1. **Personal Development**

- o Success and failure are largely determined by the causes individuals create—discipline, effort, and habits shape outcomes.

- o Mindset and emotional intelligence influence personal and professional achievements.

2. **Social and Economic Systems**

- o Societal progress or decline results from collective actions, including policies, governance, and cultural attitudes.

- o Economic stability is influenced by factors such as trade, inflation, and technological advancements.

2 Selfless Action (Nishkama Karma)

Nishkama Karma, derived from Sanskrit, refers to performing actions without any expectation of rewards or personal gains. It is a core principle in Hindu philosophy, particularly emphasized in the Bhagavad Gita. Lord Krishna advises Arjuna to act with devotion and duty, without attachment to the results. This philosophy extends beyond religious teachings, influencing ethical conduct, psychological well-being, and leadership principles. In this discussion, we explore the significance, applications, and impact of selfless action in various domains.

Philosophical Foundations of Nishkama Karma

1. Bhagavad Gita's Teachings

- The Bhagavad Gita, one of Hinduism's most revered texts, advocates for action without desire for personal gains.

- Verse (2.47): "Karmanye vadhikaraste, ma phaleshu kadachana" translates to "You have the right to perform your duty, but you are not entitled to the fruits of your actions."

- Lord Krishna explains that attachment to results leads to suffering, whereas selfless action brings peace and liberation.

2. Difference Between Nishkama Karma and Sakama Karma

- **Sakama Karma**: Actions driven by desires for outcomes.

- **Nishkama Karma**: Actions performed for duty, righteousness, or selfless service.

- The latter leads to mental tranquility and freedom from worldly bondage.

3. Connection with Dharma and Moksha

- In Hindu philosophy, Dharma (righteous duty) aligns with Nishkama Karma.

- Performing selfless action leads to inner purification, ultimately aiding in attaining Moksha (liberation).

Psychological and Ethical Dimensions

1. Psychological Benefits

- Engaging in selfless action reduces stress and anxiety by eliminating the pressure of results.

- Encourages mindfulness, allowing individuals to focus on the present.

- Enhances intrinsic motivation and personal satisfaction.

2. Ethical and Moral Implications

- Encourages honesty, fairness, and integrity in decision-making.

- Promotes altruistic behavior, leading to a more compassionate society.

Scientific Perspective on Selfless Action

1. Neuroscience and Altruism

- Studies suggest that acts of kindness trigger the release of dopamine and oxytocin, promoting happiness and emotional well-being.

- Selfless individuals tend to have lower stress levels and better social relationships.

2. Behavioral Psychology and Nishkama Karma

- Reinforces positive behavior through intrinsic motivation rather than external rewards.

- Helps build resilience and adaptability by reducing dependence on external validation.

Practical Applications of Nishkama Karma

1. Leadership and Workplace Ethics

- Leaders practicing selfless action foster a positive work culture.

- Encourages teamwork, cooperation, and ethical decision-making.

2. Personal Development

- Cultivates patience, humility, and gratitude.

- Helps individuals navigate failures and setbacks with a balanced mindset.

3. Social and Community Service

- Volunteer work and charity embody Nishkama Karma.

- Acts of service contribute to societal well-being without personal gain.

Examples of Selfless Action in History

1. Mahatma Gandhi

- Advocated non-violence and selfless service, leading India's independence movement without personal aspirations.

2. Mother Teresa

- Dedicated her life to serving the underprivileged without expecting recognition.

3. Modern Corporate Social Responsibility (CSR)

- Companies investing in social welfare initiatives without direct financial benefits embody selfless service.

Practical Steps to Cultivate Nishkama Karma

1. **Perform Duties Without Attachment**

   o Focus on the process rather than the outcome.

2. **Engage in Acts of Service**

   o Volunteer for social causes without expecting recognition.

3. **Practice Mindfulness and Detachment**

   o Meditate to cultivate a selfless mindset.

4. **Adopt a Gratitude-Oriented Life**

   o Appreciate efforts rather than results.

3 Reincarnation: The Cycle of Birth and Death

Reincarnation, also known as transmigration or rebirth, is a fundamental concept in many spiritual traditions, particularly in Hinduism, Buddhism, Jainism, and certain other philosophies. It is the belief that after death, the soul or consciousness is reborn into a new form, continuing its journey through different lives based on past actions. This process, known as **samsara**, is driven by **karma**—the accumulated consequences of one's actions in previous lives. Liberation from this endless cycle, known as **moksha** (in Hinduism and Jainism) or **nirvana** (in

Buddhism), represents the ultimate goal of spiritual evolution.

This discussion explores the principles of reincarnation, the role of karma in determining rebirth, the different realms of existence, and how one can transcend the cycle of birth and death through spiritual practice.

The Concept of Reincarnation Across Traditions

1. Hinduism and Rebirth

Hindu philosophy holds that the soul (Atman) is eternal and takes birth in different bodies across lifetimes. The Bhagavad Gita states:

"Just as a person discards old clothes and wears new ones, so does the soul discard old bodies and enter new ones." (Bhagavad Gita 2.22)

The process of reincarnation is guided by the law of karma, and a soul's next birth is influenced by its actions in previous lives. Hindu scriptures also describe different **lokas** (realms of existence) where a soul can be reborn, including heavenly, earthly, and lower realms.

2. Buddhism and the Six Realms of Existence

Buddhism expands on reincarnation through the concept of the **Six Realms of Existence**, representing different states of rebirth:

1. **Deva (Gods)** – A blissful but impermanent state of pleasure.

2. **Asura (Demi-Gods)** – A realm of power, competition, and jealousy.

3. **Manushya (Humans)** – Considered the most favorable realm for spiritual progress, as it offers a balance of suffering and wisdom.

4. **Tiryak (Animals)** – A realm dominated by ignorance, instinct, and survival.

5. **Preta (Hungry Ghosts)** – A state of insatiable desire and attachment.

6. **Naraka (Hell Beings)** – A realm of immense suffering due to past negative karma.

Unlike Hinduism, which believes in an eternal soul, Buddhism emphasizes **Anatta** (non-self), meaning that there is no permanent soul, but rather a continuity of consciousness influenced by past karma.

3. Jainism and the Doctrine of Rebirth

Jainism teaches that the soul (Jiva) is bound by karmic particles and undergoes endless rebirths until it attains **Kevala Jnana** (pure knowledge) and liberation. Jains believe in self-discipline, non-violence, and asceticism as the means to end the cycle of rebirth.

4. Western and Abrahamic Perspectives

While reincarnation is not a dominant belief in Christianity, Islam, or Judaism, some sects and mystical traditions, such as Kabbalah and Sufism, suggest the possibility of rebirth. In recent times, concepts like past-life regression and near-death experiences have fueled Western interest in reincarnation.

The Role of Karma in Reincarnation

1. Types of Karma Influencing Rebirth

In Hindu and Buddhist traditions, karma plays a decisive role in determining the circumstances of one's next life. There are three main types of karma:

- **Sanchita Karma**: The accumulated karma from all past lives.

- **Prarabdha Karma**: The portion of karma that influences the current life.

- **Kriyamana Karma**: The actions performed in the present, shaping future experiences.

2. How Karma Determines Rebirth

Every action—whether physical, mental, or verbal—creates an imprint that influences future rebirths. A virtuous life leads to a higher rebirth, while negative actions result in suffering. This principle encourages ethical living and mindfulness in one's deeds.

The Realms of Rebirth and Their Symbolism

1. Celestial Realms (Higher Spiritual Planes)

- Associated with **good karma and virtuous deeds**.

- Temporary rewards, as even gods must eventually be reborn.

2. Human Realm (Manushya Loka)

- The most desirable for spiritual growth.

- Offers free will, moral dilemmas, and the opportunity to seek enlightenment.

3. Lower Realms (Animal, Preta, and Hell Realms)

- **Animal realm**: Driven by survival instincts, ignorance, and suffering.

- **Hungry Ghost realm**: Symbolizes greed, attachment, and dissatisfaction.

- **Hell realm**: Represents immense suffering as a result of past negative karma.

Breaking Free from the Cycle: The Path to Liberation

1. Hindu Perspective: Attaining Moksha

- Following **Dharma (righteous duty)** and practicing **Bhakti (devotion)**, **Jnana (knowledge)**, and **Karma Yoga (selfless action)**.

- Renouncing material attachments and ego.

2. Buddhist Path to Nirvana

- Following the **Eightfold Path**, including right action, mindfulness, and meditation.

- Understanding the impermanence of self and reality.

3. Jain Approach to Liberation

- Practicing **Ahimsa (non-violence)**, **Aparigraha (non-attachment)**, and **Asceticism**.

- Following strict discipline to purify karma.

Scientific and Psychological Perspectives on Reincarnation

1. Studies on Past-Life Memories

- Cases of children recalling past lives, studied by researchers like Dr. Ian Stevenson.

- Evidence of past-life regression therapy showing emotional healing.

2. Psychological Interpretations

- Some theories suggest that past-life memories could be stored in the subconscious mind.

- Reincarnation beliefs provide comfort and a sense of continuity.

Modern-Day Relevance of Reincarnation Beliefs

1. Ethical Living

- Encourages individuals to lead a moral and responsible life.

2. Spiritual Growth

- Motivates self-improvement and introspection.

3. Scientific and Philosophical Exploration

- Continues to inspire research in consciousness studies and metaphysics.

4 Escaping the Cycle of Birth and Death

The ultimate goal in many spiritual traditions is to break free from the cycle of birth and death, known as samsara, and attain liberation—whether it be moksha in Hinduism, nirvana in Buddhism, or enlightenment in various philosophical traditions. The belief that the soul undergoes repeated cycles of birth, death, and rebirth is deeply embedded in Eastern religious thought. Liberation is achieved when an individual overcomes ignorance, desires, and attachments, realizing their true divine nature. This process requires a profound transformation of consciousness and adherence to specific spiritual paths that facilitate transcendence beyond material existence.

Understanding Samsara: The Endless Cycle of Rebirth

Samsara, the cycle of birth and death, is driven by karma—the law of cause and effect. According to Hindu and Buddhist philosophies, an individual's actions in one life determine the conditions of their subsequent existence. The cycle continues indefinitely until one attains liberation.

1. **Hindu Perspective on Samsara**

   o In Hinduism, samsara is viewed as a process of learning and purification. The soul (Atman) transmigrates through various lifetimes, experiencing joys and sufferings based on past karma. The ultimate goal is to realize one's true self

(Atman) as identical to the divine reality (Brahman), thus escaping the cycle.

2. **Buddhist Perspective on Samsara**

   o Buddhism perceives samsara as a state of suffering caused by attachment and ignorance. The Buddha taught that life is characterized by impermanence (anicca), suffering (dukkha), and the non-self (anatta). Liberation, or nirvana, is attained by extinguishing desire and ignorance through disciplined practice.

3. **Jain and Sikh Views on Samsara**

   o Jainism teaches that the soul accumulates karmic particles due to actions, binding it to the cycle of birth and death. Only through strict self-discipline and non-violence can one attain kevala jnana (absolute knowledge) and liberation.

   o Sikhism emphasizes devotion to God, righteous living, and selfless service as means to transcend the cycle of rebirth and merge with the divine.

Paths to Liberation

Different traditions propose various paths to escape samsara, each catering to diverse spiritual inclinations. Hinduism classifies these into four major yogic paths, while Buddhism offers the Noble Eightfold Path as a means to enlightenment.

1. Jnana Yoga (Path of Knowledge)

Jnana Yoga is the pursuit of self-inquiry and wisdom, leading to the realization that the self (Atman) is one with the absolute reality (Brahman). This path requires:

- **Scriptural study** (shravana) to understand Vedantic teachings.

- **Reflection** (manana) to contemplate the truths learned.

- **Meditation** (nididhyasana) to internalize knowledge and dissolve the ego.

- Renunciation of worldly illusions (maya) to achieve self-realization.

2. Bhakti Yoga (Path of Devotion)

Bhakti Yoga emphasizes surrendering to a higher power and cultivating unconditional love for the divine. It is practiced through:

- **Chanting and singing hymns** to foster a deep emotional connection with God.

- **Prayer and rituals** to express devotion.

- **Selfless service (seva)** as an offering to the divine.

- Developing virtues such as humility, patience, and forgiveness.

3. Karma Yoga (Path of Selfless Action)

Karma Yoga advocates performing duties without attachment to results. According to the Bhagavad Gita, selfless action purifies the soul and liberates one from karma's bondage. It includes:

- **Acting with detachment** from rewards and consequences.

- **Serving humanity** without seeking personal gain.

- **Living ethically and virtuously**, ensuring that one's actions align with dharma (righteousness).

4. Raja Yoga (Path of Meditation)

Raja Yoga involves mental discipline and meditation to achieve self-realization. It follows the eightfold path of Patanjali's Yoga Sutras:

- **Yama (ethical restraints)** – Non-violence, truthfulness, and self-discipline.

- **Niyama (self-discipline)** – Contentment, cleanliness, and devotion.

- **Asana (postures)** – Physical postures for health and stability.

- **Pranayama (breath control)** – Regulating breath to control energy.

- **Pratyahara (withdrawal of senses)** – Turning inward to focus on the self.

- **Dharana (concentration)** – Developing focus and mental clarity.

- **Dhyana (meditation)** – Deep meditation to transcend duality.

- **Samadhi (absorption)** – Ultimate realization of oneness with the divine.

The Buddhist Path to Nirvana

Buddhism provides a systematic approach to escaping samsara through the **Four Noble Truths** and the **Noble Eightfold Path**:

- **Four Noble Truths**:

    1. Suffering (dukkha) is inherent in life.

    2. The cause of suffering is attachment and desire.

    3. Cessation of suffering is possible.

    4. The path to cessation is the Noble Eightfold Path.

- **The Noble Eightfold Path**:

    o **Right View**: Understanding suffering and karma.

    o **Right Intention**: Cultivating thoughts of kindness and renunciation.

    o **Right Speech**: Avoiding falsehood and harmful words.

    o **Right Action**: Living ethically and non-violently.

    o **Right Livelihood**: Choosing a profession that aligns with morality.

- o **Right Effort**: Striving for positive mental states.

- o **Right Mindfulness**: Developing awareness of thoughts and emotions.

- o **Right Concentration**: Meditative absorption leading to enlightenment.

Obstacles to Liberation

Despite having clear paths to liberation, many challenges prevent individuals from transcending samsara:

- **Attachment and Desires**: Clinging to material possessions, relationships, and ego-based identity.

- **Ignorance (Avidya)**: Lack of awareness about the true nature of reality.

- **Karmic Burdens**: Past actions influencing present life circumstances.

- **Mind's Restlessness**: Difficulty in meditation and self-discipline.

Overcoming these obstacles requires constant self-awareness, spiritual discipline, and surrender to the divine or the ultimate truth.

5 The Scientific and Philosophical Perspectives

The nature of existence, consciousness, and the laws governing reality have been central concerns of both science and philosophy for centuries. While scientific inquiry seeks to understand the physical mechanisms that govern the universe, philosophy explores the deeper meaning and implications of these discoveries. The interplay between scientific and philosophical perspectives has given rise to profound questions about causality, determinism, free will, and the nature of consciousness. This paper explores these perspectives, addressing key theories, debates, and their implications for our understanding of reality.

Scientific Perspectives

Science relies on empirical observation, experimentation, and logical reasoning to explain phenomena. Several branches of science provide unique insights into the nature of existence and causality.

1. Physics and the Nature of Reality

Physics has played a crucial role in shaping our understanding of the universe. Several fundamental principles define how cause and effect operate in nature.

- **Classical Mechanics:** Isaac Newton's laws of motion established deterministic causality, where every action has an equal and opposite reaction. This view suggested that, given enough information, the future could be predicted with certainty.

- **Quantum Mechanics:** The advent of quantum physics challenged deterministic views. Werner Heisenberg's Uncertainty Principle states that it is impossible to measure both the position and momentum of a particle with absolute precision, introducing a probabilistic nature to reality.

- **Relativity Theory:** Albert Einstein's theory of relativity revealed that space and time are interconnected, further complicating the cause-and-effect relationship. The notion of time dilation suggests that time is not an absolute constant but is affected by gravity and motion.

2. Neuroscience and Consciousness

The study of the brain has led to significant discoveries about human cognition, perception, and consciousness.

- **Determinism in Brain Function:** Some neuroscientists argue that human decisions are a product of brain chemistry and neural activity, leaving little room for free will.

- **The Hard Problem of Consciousness:** Philosopher David Chalmers introduced this term to describe the challenge of explaining subjective experiences. While neuroscience can track brain activity, it struggles to explain why and how consciousness arises from neural processes.

- **Emergent Theories:** Some researchers propose that consciousness is an emergent property of complex systems, meaning it arises from the interaction of simpler elements rather than existing as a fundamental property of the universe.

3. Biology and Evolution

Biology explores the origins of life, adaptation, and the role of natural selection in shaping species.

- **Evolutionary Determinism:** Charles Darwin's theory of evolution suggests that all life forms are shaped by natural selection, where survival and reproduction dictate genetic propagation.

- **Genetic Influence on Behavior:** Studies in genetics indicate that behaviors and predispositions are encoded in DNA, supporting a deterministic view of human actions.

- **Epigenetics and Environmental Influence:** Modern biology also acknowledges that gene expression can be influenced by environmental factors, suggesting a more complex interaction between determinism and free will.

Philosophical Perspectives

Philosophy offers deeper inquiries into the implications of scientific discoveries, raising fundamental questions about existence and reality.

1. Metaphysics and the Nature of Reality

Metaphysics explores the fundamental nature of reality, existence, and causality.

- **Materialism vs. Idealism:** Materialism argues that physical matter is the only reality, while idealism asserts that reality is shaped by consciousness.

- **Dualism:** Proposed by René Descartes, dualism suggests that mind and body are separate entities, with consciousness existing independently of the physical world.

- **Panpsychism:** This theory posits that consciousness is a fundamental aspect of the universe, existing even in subatomic particles.

2. Free Will vs. Determinism

The debate over free will and determinism has significant ethical and existential implications.

- **Hard Determinism:** Asserts that all events, including human actions, are determined by previous causes, negating the possibility of free will.

- **Libertarian Free Will:** Argues that individuals have the capacity to make choices independent of deterministic forces.

- **Compatibilism:** Suggests that free will and determinism can coexist, meaning human choices are influenced by prior causes but are still made voluntarily.

3. Ethics and Moral Responsibility

The concept of moral responsibility is closely tied to debates about free will and determinism.

- **Utilitarianism:** A moral philosophy that evaluates actions based on their consequences, aligning closely with a scientific view of cause and effect.

- **Deontology:** Asserts that actions are morally right or wrong regardless of consequences, suggesting an innate moral law beyond deterministic causes.

- **Existentialism:** Emphasizes individual freedom and responsibility, arguing that humans create their own meaning through choices.

Bridging Science and Philosophy

While science provides empirical data and testable theories, philosophy helps interpret these findings, leading to a more comprehensive understanding of reality.

- **The Simulation Hypothesis:** Some scientists and philosophers propose that reality may be a simulation, challenging traditional notions of existence.

- **The Anthropic Principle:** Suggests that the universe's physical constants are fine-tuned for life, raising philosophical and theological questions.

- **The Role of Artificial Intelligence:** As AI advances, questions about machine consciousness, ethics, and the nature of intelligence become increasingly relevant.

6 Moral and Ethical Implications

Morality and ethics are fundamental aspects of human society, shaping our decisions, behaviors, and interactions. The concepts of right and wrong, justice, and virtue have been explored by philosophers, religious traditions, and legal systems throughout history. Ethical considerations guide personal conduct, professional responsibilities, and societal norms, influencing everything from individual choices to global policies. This document delves into the moral and ethical implications of human actions from various perspectives, including philosophy, psychology, law, and contemporary issues.

Philosophical Foundations of Morality and Ethics

1. Deontological Ethics

- Proposed by Immanuel Kant, deontology asserts that actions are morally right or wrong based on rules and duties rather than consequences.

- Moral obligations, such as honesty and fairness, are absolute and must be followed regardless of outcomes.

- Criticism: Deontological ethics may lead to rigid moral judgments that disregard situational complexities.

2. Utilitarianism

- Introduced by Jeremy Bentham and John Stuart Mill, utilitarianism suggests that moral actions are those that maximize overall happiness and minimize suffering.

- The principle of "the greatest good for the greatest number" guides decision-making.

- Criticism: It can justify morally questionable actions if they lead to a net positive outcome.

3. Virtue Ethics

- Rooted in Aristotle's philosophy, virtue ethics focuses on character development and cultivating virtues such as courage, kindness, and wisdom.

- Rather than following fixed rules, moral individuals act virtuously in different circumstances.

- Criticism: Lacks clear guidelines for resolving moral dilemmas.

4. Ethics of Care

- Emphasizes relationships and the moral significance of care, empathy, and compassion.

- Developed in feminist ethics, it challenges traditional ethical theories that prioritize justice over care.

- Criticism: Can be seen as subjective and lacking universal applicability.

Psychological Perspectives on Moral Decision-Making

1. **Moral Development (Kohlberg's Stages)**

   - Preconventional: Morality is based on consequences (reward vs. punishment).

   - Conventional: Morality is influenced by societal rules and expectations.

   - Postconventional: Morality is based on abstract principles and ethical reasoning.

2. **The Role of Emotions**

o   Emotions like guilt, empathy, and disgust significantly influence moral judgments.

o   Studies in neuroscience show that moral decision-making involves brain regions like the prefrontal cortex and amygdala.

3. **Moral Relativism vs. Moral Absolutism**

o   Moral relativism argues that moral principles vary across cultures and contexts.

o   Moral absolutism maintains that certain moral truths are universal and unchanging.

Moral and Ethical Implications in Various Domains

1. Medical Ethics

- Issues like euthanasia, abortion, organ donation, and genetic engineering raise ethical dilemmas.

- The principle of "do no harm" (non-maleficence) and patient autonomy guide medical decisions.

2. Business Ethics

- Corporate social responsibility (CSR), fair labor practices, and ethical consumerism shape business morality.

- Ethical dilemmas include corruption, environmental impact, and employee rights.

3. Legal and Criminal Justice Ethics

- Balancing justice with rehabilitation in legal systems.

- Ethical concerns in law enforcement, capital punishment, and prisoners' rights.

4. Technology and Artificial Intelligence Ethics

- Ethical implications of AI, data privacy, surveillance, and automation.

- Concerns over bias in AI decision-making and accountability.

5. Environmental Ethics

- Climate change, conservation, and sustainable practices raise moral questions about humanity's responsibility toward nature.

- Concepts like deep ecology and ecofeminism advocate for a more ethical approach to environmental stewardship.

Contemporary Moral Dilemmas

1. **Bioethics and Genetic Engineering**

   - CRISPR technology allows genetic modification but raises ethical concerns about "designer babies."

   - Debates over cloning and genetic privacy.

2. **Social Justice and Human Rights**

- o Equality, racism, gender rights, and LGBTQ+ rights are central ethical issues in modern society.

- o Movements advocating for social change challenge existing moral frameworks.

3. **War and Peace Ethics**

- o Just war theory vs. pacifism.

- o Ethical concerns about nuclear weapons, drone warfare, and military interventions.

Conclusion

Karma and reincarnation present a profound understanding of human existence, emphasizing personal responsibility, ethical living, and spiritual evolution. The law of cause and effect ensures that every action has consequences, while the cycle of rebirth provides opportunities for growth and redemption. By practicing selfless action, seeking knowledge, and cultivating devotion, one can transcend the cycle of birth and death, ultimately attaining liberation.

These timeless concepts continue to inspire philosophical inquiry, scientific exploration, and moral reflection, offering guidance for leading a purposeful and meaningful life.

Chapter 08: Leadership and Ethics: Lessons from the Gita

Introduction

The Bhagavad Gita, one of the most revered scriptures in Hindu philosophy, provides profound insights into leadership, ethics, and governance. Delivered by Lord Krishna to Arjuna on the battlefield of Kurukshetra, the Gita serves as a timeless guide for making ethical decisions and leading with wisdom and integrity. In today's complex world, leaders in business, governance, and society can draw invaluable lessons from Krishna's teachings. This essay explores the Gita's guidance on ethical decision-making, essential leadership qualities, and the application of its wisdom in business and governance.

1 Ethical Decision-Making: The Gita's Guidance

The Principle of Dharma (Righteous Duty)

At the heart of the Bhagavad Gita is the concept of *Dharma*, which refers to one's duty and righteousness. Krishna advises Arjuna to perform his duty as a warrior without being swayed by personal emotions. In leadership, this translates into making decisions based on principles rather than personal interests or external pressures. Leaders must prioritize ethics, fairness, and the greater good over individual or organizational gains.

Understanding Dharma

Dharma is a multifaceted concept encompassing righteousness, justice, morality, and duty. It is not a rigid set of rules but a dynamic principle that adapts to the context and responsibilities of an individual. In the Gita, Krishna explains that every person has a unique duty based on their role in society, and fulfilling this duty with sincerity and integrity is the highest form of righteousness.

Dharma in Leadership

Leaders in various fields face ethical dilemmas where personal biases, external influences, or short-term gains may cloud their judgment. The Gita emphasizes that a true leader must remain steadfast in their principles and act in the best interest of their people. Krishna tells Arjuna:

"It is better to live your own destiny imperfectly than to live an imitation of somebody else's life with perfection." (Bhagavad Gita 3.35)

This verse highlights the importance of staying true to one's responsibilities rather than succumbing to external pressures or imitating others. A leader must understand their unique role and fulfill it with dedication, regardless of the challenges.

Balancing Personal and Professional Dharma

In real-life situations, conflicts often arise between personal and professional duties. The Gita teaches that ethical leadership requires balancing these responsibilities while adhering to moral values. For instance, a corporate leader may have to make difficult decisions that affect employees, stakeholders, and the environment. By following the principle of Dharma, they can ensure that their decisions are fair, transparent, and in alignment with long-term well-being.

Practical Applications in Governance and Business

- **Policy-making:** Ethical governance should be based on justice and the welfare of all citizens, much like Krishna's guidance to Arjuna.

- **Corporate Leadership:** Business leaders should focus on long-term value creation rather than short-term profits, ensuring sustainability and ethical conduct.

- **Personal Integrity:** Leaders must cultivate self-discipline and moral strength to act with conviction and fairness.

By embracing Dharma, leaders can navigate complex situations with clarity and integrity, fostering a culture of ethical leadership in society.

Nishkama Karma: Selfless Action

Nishkama Karma, a fundamental teaching of the Bhagavad Gita, emphasizes performing one's duty without attachment to the outcomes. Krishna advises Arjuna to act with dedication but without expectation of rewards, explaining that true fulfillment comes from the process of righteous action rather than its results. In leadership, this principle teaches that ethical leaders should focus on their responsibilities with sincerity, without being driven by personal ambition or external validation. Nishkama Karma fosters a mindset of service and commitment, encouraging leaders to work for the collective good rather than selfish gains. This philosophy is particularly relevant in governance and business, where decision-makers often face pressures to prioritize short-term profits over long-term sustainability. Leaders who embody Nishkama Karma make choices based on ethical considerations, ensuring that their actions benefit society rather than serving their interests alone. Moreover, this principle cultivates resilience, as leaders who are detached from success and failure remain steadfast in their values, making rational decisions even in adversity. The modern corporate world can significantly benefit from this mindset, as it promotes fairness, integrity, and responsibility among employees and executives. Additionally, Nishkama Karma aligns with the concept of servant leadership, where the leader's primary role is to serve others, fostering an organizational culture of trust and collaboration. By practicing selfless action, leaders can inspire their teams, enhance employee engagement, and create sustainable growth. This approach is not about renouncing material success but about working with a sense of duty and contribution rather than mere personal gain. The Gita thus offers a transformative perspective on leadership—where success is redefined as the ability to lead with purpose, ethics, and unwavering commitment to the greater good.

Equanimity in Decision-Making

One of the most profound teachings of the Bhagavad Gita is *Samatvam,* or equanimity—the ability to remain balanced in both success and failure. Krishna advises

Arjuna to develop a mindset that is unaffected by external circumstances, enabling him to make rational, ethical, and effective decisions. Equanimity in decision-making is crucial for leaders in all fields, as it helps them navigate challenges with clarity and composure.

In leadership, maintaining equanimity allows decision-makers to stay focused on long-term goals without being swayed by short-term gains or emotional reactions. A leader who practices *Samatvam* is neither elated by success nor distressed by failure, ensuring that their choices are guided by wisdom rather than impulse. This quality fosters resilience, as leaders who cultivate inner stability can face adversity without losing their moral compass.

Krishna's teaching emphasizes that true leaders should not be attached to praise or criticism but should act with a sense of duty and integrity. This principle is especially relevant in corporate and political governance, where leaders often face pressure from various stakeholders. By practicing equanimity, they can make unbiased and ethical decisions that benefit the larger community rather than catering to personal or political interests.

The modern business environment, with its volatility and unpredictability, demands leaders who can remain composed under pressure. Executives who embody *Samatvam* are better equipped to handle crises, negotiate conflicts, and lead organizations through uncertainty. This mindset also fosters ethical behavior, as leaders who are not driven by ego or external validation are more likely to prioritize values over personal gain.

Furthermore, Krishna teaches that equanimity leads to inner peace, which enhances mental clarity and decision-making abilities. Leaders who cultivate this trait can create a positive and stable work culture, inspiring their teams to remain focused and motivated despite external challenges.

By integrating the principle of *Samatvam* into their leadership approach, decision-makers can develop the resilience, wisdom, and ethical clarity needed to guide their organizations and societies toward long-term success and stability.

2 Leadership Qualities from Krishna's Teachings

The Bhagavad Gita, one of the most revered scriptures in Hindu philosophy, provides profound insights into leadership, ethics, and governance. Delivered by Lord Krishna to Arjuna on the battlefield of Kurukshetra, the Gita serves as a timeless guide for making ethical decisions and leading with wisdom and integrity. In today's complex world, leaders in business, governance, and society can draw invaluable lessons from Krishna's teachings. This essay explores the Gita's guidance on ethical decision-making, essential leadership qualities, and the application of its wisdom in business and governance.

Ethical Decision-Making: The Gita's Guidance

1. Vision and Strategic Thinking

A great leader must possess a clear vision and the ability to anticipate future challenges. Krishna, as a divine strategist, meticulously planned every step of the Mahabharata war with foresight and wisdom. His ability to foresee the consequences of actions, prepare for challenges, and guide his allies toward victory demonstrates the essence of strategic thinking.

Leaders in governance and business must develop strategic thinking skills to guide their organizations through uncertain times. A well-defined vision provides direction, inspires teams, and ensures sustainable growth. Strategic leaders analyze risks, consider long-term implications, and make informed decisions. In today's dynamic world, where industries and economies evolve rapidly, leaders must adopt Krishna's approach by staying adaptable, planning ahead, and making ethical choices that benefit society.

Successful businesses are built on visionary leadership. Founders and CEOs like Steve Jobs, Elon Musk, and Satya Nadella exemplify how foresight and strategic thinking drive innovation and long-term success. Similarly, political leaders who navigate crises effectively often possess the ability to think beyond the present moment, aligning their actions with a larger goal.

2. Leading by Example (*Yatharth Karma*)

Krishna emphasizes that a leader should lead by example. He demonstrated this principle throughout the Mahabharata by actively participating in the war, not as a warrior but as a guide and charioteer. His actions highlighted the importance of responsibility, humility, and ethical leadership.

In organizations, ethical leadership inspires employees to adopt similar values. A leader who upholds integrity, discipline, and responsibility cultivates a culture of ethical behavior within their team. Employees look up to their leaders as role models, and their behavior significantly influences organizational culture. When leaders demonstrate honesty, accountability, and fairness, they instill trust and loyalty among their teams.

Corporate scandals, such as the Enron and Volkswagen emissions cases, highlight the dangers of unethical leadership. In contrast, leaders like Ratan Tata and Warren Buffett are revered for their commitment to ethical business practices, transparency, and employee well-being. Krishna's teaching reminds us that genuine leadership is not about authority but about setting an example through actions, ensuring that followers embrace the same values.

3. Adaptability and Crisis Management

One of Krishna's greatest strengths was his ability to adapt to different situations. Whether as a charioteer, a diplomat, or a guide, Krishna's approach changed based on circumstances. This adaptability is a crucial trait for modern leaders, who must navigate unpredictable challenges in a rapidly evolving business and political landscape.

Effective crisis management requires the ability to think on one's feet, assess situations objectively, and respond with wisdom. Leaders must remain calm under pressure, seek creative solutions, and make decisions that align with their organization's values. The COVID-19 pandemic illustrated how companies and governments had to pivot quickly, adapting to new challenges in remote work, healthcare management, and economic stability.

Krishna's role in the Mahabharata war provides valuable lessons in crisis management. He turned potential setbacks into opportunities by ensuring that his strategies were flexible. Whether negotiating peace before the war or offering tactical advice during battle, he demonstrated the power of resilience and quick thinking. Leaders who embrace adaptability can successfully steer their organizations through crises, ensuring long-term sustainability.

4. Compassion and Emotional Intelligence

While Krishna was a strategic leader, he was also compassionate and deeply connected with those around him. His ability to understand Arjuna's inner turmoil and provide him with guidance reflects the importance of emotional intelligence in leadership.

In the modern workplace, emotional intelligence is essential for leaders to build strong relationships, foster teamwork, and create a positive work environment. A leader who understands employees' emotions, listens actively, and responds with empathy earns respect and loyalty. Research has shown that organizations led by emotionally intelligent leaders have higher employee satisfaction, reduced turnover rates, and improved overall performance.

Leaders like Mahatma Gandhi, Nelson Mandela, and Jacinda Ardern have demonstrated how compassion can transform societies. Their ability to connect with people, understand their struggles, and lead with empathy made them extraordinary figures in history. Krishna's approach reminds us that true leadership is not just about making decisions but also about uplifting those who follow.

5. Fearlessness and Courage

Krishna teaches that true leaders should be fearless in upholding righteousness. Courage is essential for making difficult decisions, standing up against injustice, and staying true to one's principles, even in adversity.

Leaders often face criticism, competition, and uncertainty. The ability to remain steadfast in one's beliefs and take bold actions defines great leadership. Whether in politics, business, or social movements, history has witnessed fearless leaders who changed the world.

Krishna's advice to Arjuna—to fight for righteousness without fear—illustrates this principle. In corporate leadership, figures like Jeff Bezos and Indra Nooyi took bold risks that led to groundbreaking innovations. Political leaders like Abraham Lincoln and Winston Churchill showcased unwavering courage in times of crisis, leading their nations through immense challenges.

Fearless leadership also means taking responsibility for failures and learning from mistakes. Krishna's wisdom teaches that setbacks are temporary and that resilience and determination pave the way for future success.

3 Applying Gita's Wisdom in Business and Governance

The Bhagavad Gita, one of the most revered spiritual and philosophical texts, offers timeless wisdom that extends beyond personal spirituality to influence leadership, business ethics, and governance. Krishna's teachings emphasize righteous conduct, selfless service, and ethical decision-making—principles that are highly relevant in today's corporate and political spheres. This document explores how the teachings of the Gita can guide ethical business practices, just governance, and the balance between material success and spiritual values.

Ethical Business Practices

Honesty, Transparency, and Accountability

The Bhagavad Gita teaches that righteousness (*dharma*) must be the foundation of all actions. In the business world, this translates to operating with honesty, transparency, and accountability. Ethical business practices foster trust among stakeholders, including employees, customers, investors, and society at large. Organizations that prioritize integrity build strong reputations and long-term sustainability.

In contrast, businesses that engage in unethical practices such as fraud, corruption, or deception may achieve short-term gains but ultimately suffer in the long run. Krishna's guidance to Arjuna in the Gita highlights the importance of performing one's duties without deceit and selfish motives, a lesson that can be applied to ethical leadership in corporations.

Corporate Social Responsibility (CSR)

The Gita emphasizes selfless service (*nishkama karma*), which aligns with the modern concept of Corporate Social Responsibility (CSR). Krishna teaches that one should act for the benefit of others without attachment to personal gain. Businesses that integrate CSR into their core strategy contribute to the greater good, ensuring sustainability, environmental protection, and social welfare.

Successful companies like Tata Group and Microsoft actively invest in CSR initiatives, demonstrating that businesses can be both profitable and socially responsible. By following Krishna's teachings, organizations can align their goals with the well-being of society while maintaining financial success.

Ethical Leadership and Decision-Making

Leadership in business requires making difficult decisions that affect employees, customers, and the broader community. The Gita encourages leaders to act based on *dharma* (righteousness) rather than greed, fear, or personal bias. Ethical decision-making ensures fairness, transparency, and justice, which strengthen organizational culture and long-term stability.

A leader who follows Krishna's principles avoids unethical shortcuts and instead focuses on sustainable growth, employee welfare, and corporate integrity. This approach not only benefits businesses but also enhances their social impact.

Governance Based on Justice and Fairness

Krishna's Role as a Just Leader

Krishna's role in the Mahabharata war showcases his unwavering commitment to justice and fairness. He guided the Pandavas in their struggle against oppression while ensuring that their actions aligned with ethical principles. This lesson is particularly relevant for modern governance, where policymakers must balance power, justice, and societal welfare.

Good governance is rooted in fairness, impartiality, and the welfare of all citizens. Krishna's leadership exemplifies the principles of equitable decision-making, which can serve as a model for contemporary political leaders.

Ethical Policy-Making

Governance should prioritize ethical policies that promote equality, justice, and social well-being. The Gita teaches that leaders must make decisions based on the collective good rather than personal gain. Governments that implement policies supporting education, healthcare, economic stability, and environmental sustainability reflect Krishna's teachings on responsible leadership.

For instance, policies that protect marginalized communities, ensure fair wages, and regulate corporate accountability align with the Gita's ethical framework. By following Krishna's wisdom, policymakers can foster social harmony and sustainable development.

The Role of Leaders in Governance

Krishna advises leaders to act with selflessness and commitment to duty. He reminds Arjuna that leadership is a responsibility, not a privilege. Politicians, corporate executives, and policymakers must recognize their role as servants of society, prioritizing the needs of the people over personal ambitions.

A leader who governs with Krishna's wisdom remains free from corruption, favoritism, and ego-driven decisions. Such leadership fosters public trust, stability, and progressive development, ensuring that governance is aligned with ethical principles.

Balancing Material Success with Spiritual Values

The Gita's View on Wealth and Success

The Gita does not condemn material success but warns against attachment to wealth. Krishna teaches that prosperity should not lead to arrogance, greed, or unethical behavior. Instead, wealth should be acquired and utilized in alignment with *dharma* (righteousness).

Many successful business leaders integrate spiritual values into their corporate philosophy. Companies that embrace ethical capitalism prioritize employee well-being, sustainability, and social responsibility alongside profit maximization.

Ethical Capitalism and Sustainable Growth

The modern economic landscape often promotes profit-driven motives at the expense of ethical considerations. The Gita's teachings advocate for ethical capitalism, where businesses balance financial growth with moral responsibility.

For instance, fair trade, environmentally friendly production methods, and ethical labor practices reflect Krishna's vision of righteousness in economic activities. Businesses that align with these principles experience long-term success while contributing to societal welfare.

Detachment from Greed and Ego

Krishna advises Arjuna to perform his duty without attachment to rewards. This principle can be applied to business and governance by encouraging leaders to focus on their responsibilities rather than personal gain.

Greed-driven decisions often lead to corruption, exploitation, and unethical practices. However, leaders who embrace Krishna's wisdom prioritize fairness, sustainability, and long-term impact over short-term profits.

Work as a Form of Worship

The Gita teaches that work should be viewed as a sacred duty rather than a means to an end. In business and governance, this perspective encourages individuals to dedicate themselves to their responsibilities with sincerity, integrity, and devotion.

When leaders approach their roles with a sense of service, they contribute to a just and prosperous society. Employees who adopt this mindset find greater job satisfaction, purpose, and motivation, leading to organizational success.

Conclusion

The Bhagavad Gita provides timeless wisdom on leadership and ethics, offering valuable lessons for individuals in business, politics, and society. By following Krishna's teachings—rooted in righteousness, selfless action, and strategic wisdom—leaders can navigate challenges with integrity and effectiveness. Whether in governance or corporate leadership, applying the principles of the Gita can lead to ethical decision-making, sustainable success, and a just society.

Chapter 09: Modern Relevance of the Bhagavad Gita

Introduction

The Bhagavad Gita, a sacred Hindu scripture, has been revered for centuries as a spiritual and philosophical guide. Its teachings transcend religious boundaries and provide wisdom applicable to all aspects of life. In the 21st century, as humanity grapples with technological advancements, existential crises, and ethical dilemmas, the Gita's message remains profoundly relevant. This article explores how the Bhagavad Gita continues to shape spirituality, personal and professional life, and its intersection with modern science.

1 Spirituality in the 21st Century

In today's fast-paced world, spirituality is often overlooked in favor of material pursuits. However, the search for inner peace and purpose remains a fundamental human endeavor. The Bhagavad Gita provides valuable insights into spirituality by emphasizing self-realization, detachment, and devotion.

The Role of Dharma in Modern Life

The concept of *dharma* (duty/righteousness) is central to the Gita. It teaches individuals to perform their duties selflessly, without attachment to the results. This principle is crucial in today's world, where ethical dilemmas often arise in personal and professional spheres.

In modern life, people face conflicts between personal ambitions and social responsibilities. The Gita's message of performing duty without selfish motives can guide individuals to make ethical decisions. For example, professionals often struggle with work-life balance; adhering to the principles of *dharma* allows them to fulfill responsibilities without undue stress or guilt.

The Gita also highlights the importance of righteousness over convenience. Many people today compromise on ethics for success, but Krishna's guidance to Arjuna emphasizes that duty should always be performed with integrity and moral responsibility.

Meditation and Mindfulness

The Gita advocates meditation as a means to attain inner peace. In modern times, mindfulness and meditation have been scientifically proven to reduce stress, enhance focus, and improve overall well-being. The Gita's teachings on *dhyana yoga* align with contemporary mindfulness practices.

Meditation in the Gita is not just a relaxation technique but a path to self-realization. Krishna advises Arjuna to control his mind and senses, emphasizing that a disciplined mind leads to enlightenment. This is highly relevant in the 21st century, where stress, anxiety, and information overload dominate daily life.

Many studies support the Gita's insights on meditation. Neuroscientific research shows that meditation enhances brain function, improves emotional stability, and increases resilience. The concept of *sthita-prajna* (a steady and wise mind) resonates with modern psychological theories of emotional intelligence and mental resilience.

Overcoming Materialism and Ego

Consumerism and materialistic pursuits dominate modern society, often leading to dissatisfaction. The Gita teaches *vairagya* (detachment), encouraging individuals to seek fulfillment beyond material possessions, thus promoting a balanced and meaningful life.

Materialism is a significant source of stress and unhappiness in today's world. People often equate success with wealth and status, neglecting inner peace and personal growth. The Gita warns against attachment to transient pleasures and advocates for a life centered around higher consciousness.

Practicing detachment does not mean renouncing the world but developing an attitude of non-attachment. This can be applied in everyday life—whether in relationships, work, or financial aspirations. When individuals learn to detach from results and focus on the process, they experience greater satisfaction and peace.

Modern psychology echoes this wisdom. Studies on happiness suggest that intrinsic goals (such as personal growth, relationships, and community service) bring lasting fulfillment, while extrinsic goals (such as money and fame) often lead to temporary pleasure but long-term dissatisfaction. The Gita's teachings encourage shifting focus from materialistic desires to self-awareness and service to others.

2 The Gita's Message in Personal and Professional Life

The Bhagavad Gita is not just a religious text; it is a guide to living a life of integrity, wisdom, and resilience. Its principles can be applied in personal relationships, workplace ethics, and leadership roles.

Leadership and Decision-Making

The conversation between Lord Krishna and Arjuna on the battlefield symbolizes the dilemmas faced by leaders today. The Gita teaches that a true leader should act with wisdom, fairness, and a sense of duty, qualities essential for ethical leadership in corporate and political spheres.

Leaders today often face moral dilemmas, such as balancing profit with ethical responsibilities. The Gita provides a framework for making righteous decisions by prioritizing duty over personal gain. Ethical leadership, based on the Gita's wisdom, fosters trust, teamwork, and long-term success.

Stress Management and Emotional Stability

Modern life is filled with stress, anxiety, and uncertainty. The Gita's teachings on *karma yoga* (the path of selfless action) encourage individuals to work diligently while maintaining equanimity, reducing stress and enhancing productivity.

Understanding that results are not entirely within one's control helps individuals remain calm in challenging situations. This mindset shift is crucial for managing workplace stress, personal disappointments, and financial uncertainties.

Ethical Work Culture

The principle of *nishkama karma* (selfless action) promotes ethical conduct in the workplace. In an era where unethical practices often dominate, the Gita's emphasis on righteousness and honesty fosters a moral work environment.

Organizations that follow ethical business practices not only build a positive reputation but also ensure long-term sustainability. The Gita's guidance can help professionals make ethical choices, treat colleagues fairly, and contribute positively to society.

3 Bridging Ancient Wisdom with Modern Science

While the Bhagavad Gita is an ancient text, many of its teachings align with modern scientific discoveries, particularly in psychology, neuroscience, and quantum physics.

Neuroscience and the Gita's Concept of Mind Control

The Gita emphasizes controlling the mind to attain peace and success. Modern neuroscience supports this idea, showing that mindfulness and meditation can rewire the brain, enhancing cognitive function and emotional stability.

Scientific studies demonstrate that meditation, as advocated in the Gita, strengthens neural connections, enhances emotional intelligence, and improves focus.

The prefrontal cortex, responsible for decision-making and self-control, is significantly affected by mindfulness practices.

Krishna's advice to Arjuna about steadying the mind aligns with modern research on neuroplasticity. Neuroplasticity refers to the brain's ability to reorganize itself by forming new neural connections, proving that disciplined mental training, as suggested in the Gita, can lead to significant psychological transformations.

Additionally, the limbic system, which governs emotions, is regulated through meditation. This aligns with the Gita's idea of *sthita-prajna* (steady wisdom), where a person remains unshaken in the face of life's highs and lows.

Quantum Physics and the Concept of Reality

The Gita suggests that the material world is transient and that true existence lies beyond physical reality. This idea resonates with quantum physics, which challenges classical notions of reality and suggests the existence of multiple dimensions and interconnectedness.

In the Bhagavad Gita, Krishna describes the eternal soul (*Atman*) as separate from the perishable body. This notion parallels the quantum theory of wave-particle duality, which suggests that particles can exist in multiple states simultaneously until observed. Just as quantum mechanics posits an underlying field of energy beyond tangible matter, the Gita asserts the existence of a higher, eternal reality beyond the material world.

The famous double-slit experiment in quantum mechanics demonstrates how observation affects reality, suggesting that consciousness plays a role in shaping existence. Similarly, the Gita emphasizes that perception and awareness determine our experiences, reinforcing the idea that reality is subjective and shaped by our consciousness.

Furthermore, the principle of non-locality in quantum physics suggests that particles can influence each other instantaneously across vast distances. This concept mirrors the Gita's teaching on the interconnectedness of all beings, highlighting the unity underlying apparent diversity.

Psychology and Self-Realization

The Gita's teachings on self-awareness, detachment, and mindfulness align with modern psychological theories of self-actualization and emotional intelligence, proving its relevance in contemporary mental health studies.

The concept of *Atman* (the true self) in the Gita is akin to Carl Jung's theory of individuation, where an individual strives to integrate various aspects of their personality to achieve wholeness. The Gita encourages self-inquiry, similar to modern therapeutic approaches that promote self-awareness as a key to mental well-being.

Moreover, the idea of *detachment* (*vairagya*) in the Gita is comparable to cognitive-behavioral therapy (CBT), which helps individuals reframe negative thoughts and detach from destructive emotions. Psychological resilience, emphasized in positive psychology, aligns with the Gita's teachings on equanimity and facing challenges without losing inner peace.

The Bhagavad Gita also underscores the importance of purpose-driven living, a concept widely recognized in psychology. Viktor Frankl's *Logotherapy* emphasizes finding meaning in life as a way to overcome suffering, a philosophy that closely mirrors Krishna's advice to Arjuna about embracing duty with devotion and selflessness.

Additionally, the practice of mindfulness—rooted in Eastern traditions and widely used in modern psychotherapy—is integral to the Gita's teachings. Krishna advises constant awareness and presence in action, a practice that fosters greater emotional stability, reduces anxiety, and enhances overall well-being.

Conclusion

The Bhagavad Gita continues to be a beacon of wisdom, offering guidance in spirituality, personal growth, and professional ethics. Its teachings remain timeless, providing solutions to modern challenges and bridging the gap between ancient wisdom and scientific advancements. By integrating the Gita's principles into daily life, individuals can cultivate inner peace, resilience, and ethical leadership, ensuring a harmonious and meaningful existence in the 21st century.

Chapter 10: Conclusion: The Eternal Message of the Bhagavad Gita

Introduction: The Timeless Wisdom of the Gita

The Bhagavad Gita, often referred to as the "Song of God," is one of the most revered scriptures in Hindu philosophy. It presents a profound discourse between Lord Krishna and Arjuna on the battlefield of Kurukshetra, addressing fundamental questions about life, duty, righteousness, and the path to self-realization. The teachings of the Gita are not confined to any one era or group but hold universal relevance. They provide a guiding light to individuals seeking wisdom, clarity, and peace in the complexities of life.

Integrating Gita's Philosophy in Daily Life

Self-Realization and Inner Peace

One of the core teachings of the Bhagavad Gita is self-realization. It urges individuals to look beyond the temporary nature of the physical world and recognize the eternal soul within. This awareness fosters inner peace and helps individuals navigate life's challenges with equanimity. By cultivating a deep connection with one's true self, individuals can transcend fleeting emotions and find lasting contentment.

Detachment and Duty (Karma Yoga)

The Gita emphasizes the philosophy of Karma Yoga—selfless action performed without attachment to the results. Krishna advises Arjuna to focus on his duty as a warrior without being swayed by the fear of success or failure. In modern life, this teaching is invaluable. By committing ourselves to our responsibilities with sincerity and dedication, without obsessing over outcomes, we can achieve both efficiency and mental peace. This detachment does not mean inaction but rather an enlightened approach to work that frees us from anxiety.

The Power of Devotion (Bhakti Yoga)

Bhakti Yoga, the path of devotion, is another crucial teaching of the Gita. Krishna emphasizes that unwavering devotion and surrender to the Divine lead to liberation. In our daily lives, this principle translates to cultivating faith, humility, and love—whether towards God, a higher purpose, or humanity. Devotion fosters resilience, providing strength in times of adversity and a sense of connection with something greater than oneself.

Knowledge and Wisdom (Jnana Yoga)

Jnana Yoga, the path of knowledge, highlights the importance of wisdom in attaining liberation. Krishna encourages Arjuna to seek knowledge, question reality, and transcend ignorance. This principle is particularly relevant in today's world, where continuous learning and self-reflection help individuals grow intellectually and spiritually. By striving for deeper understanding and critical thinking, one can overcome illusions and embrace truth.

Overcoming Existential Dilemmas

Finding Clarity Amidst Confusion

The Bhagavad Gita was spoken at a time of great moral and emotional crisis for Arjuna. Similarly, individuals today often face dilemmas regarding their careers, relationships, and personal beliefs. The Gita teaches that clarity comes through introspection, guidance, and aligning one's actions with higher principles. By practicing mindfulness and meditation, one can cultivate inner stillness and make decisions with wisdom and confidence.

The Role of Dharma (Righteousness)

A central theme of the Gita is *Dharma*, or righteous duty. Krishna instructs Arjuna that performing one's duty with integrity, even when faced with hardships, is the highest virtue. This teaching is particularly relevant in the modern world, where moral ambiguity often clouds judgment. Upholding ethical values, staying true to one's principles, and fulfilling responsibilities with sincerity lead to personal fulfillment and societal harmony.

Balancing Material and Spiritual Life

The Gita does not advocate renouncing worldly life but rather finding a balance between material pursuits and spiritual growth. Krishna advises Arjuna to live in the world without being bound by it. In today's fast-paced world, maintaining this equilibrium is crucial. By integrating meditation, ethical conduct, and selfless service into daily routines, individuals can lead a life of purpose while enjoying worldly success.

Living with Purpose and Harmony

Achieving Mental Equilibrium

One of the key messages of the Bhagavad Gita is achieving mental stability amidst life's ups and downs. Krishna teaches that happiness and sorrow, gain and loss, success and failure are transient. By cultivating equanimity (*samattva*), individuals can navigate challenges without being overwhelmed. This mindset fosters resilience and helps maintain a calm, focused approach to life.

Practicing Selfless Service

The Gita encourages *Seva*, or selfless service, as a means to purify the heart and uplift society. Serving others without expectation of rewards cultivates humility and compassion. This principle is reflected in acts of kindness, charity, and contributing positively to one's community. By engaging in selfless service, individuals can create a meaningful impact while attaining personal growth.

Attaining Liberation (Moksha)

Ultimately, the Gita's teachings aim at *Moksha*, or liberation from the cycle of birth and death. This liberation is not just a metaphysical goal but also a state of inner freedom achieved by transcending ego, desires, and attachments. By following the paths of Karma Yoga, Bhakti Yoga, and Jnana Yoga, individuals can gradually dissolve ignorance and attain self-realization.

Conclusion: The Eternal Relevance of the Gita

The Bhagavad Gita remains a timeless source of wisdom, guiding humanity through the complexities of life. Its teachings offer practical solutions for personal growth, ethical dilemmas, and spiritual enlightenment. By integrating the principles of selfless action, devotion, and wisdom, individuals can lead a life of purpose, balance, and inner peace. Whether facing personal struggles or seeking deeper meaning, the eternal message of the Gita serves as a beacon of light, inspiring generations to live with courage, wisdom, and harmony.

9 7 9 8 8 9 7 7 7 4 1 2 8